A MODERN HR NOVEL

THE COMEBACK

ANNISSA DESHPANDE

Published by Loglab, LLC

ISBN: 978-1-647043-40-7 (paperback)
ISBN: 978-1-647043-39-1 (eBook)

For my *aji* (grandmother)

Smt. Usha S. Jani
February 17, 1924–December 27, 2020

CHAPTER 1

MARK FRANCIS, CEO of Dominal Industries, stood alone in his corner office late on a Monday afternoon and stared out intently at the brown trees and gray sky. He lightly banged his forehead against the large window.

It had been an unseasonably cold fall in Chicago. Even now, in early September, some trees had already shed leaves, revealing the first barren branches of autumn.

Mark shuddered, turning from the window to see financial reports strewn across the mahogany executive desk of the retired Dominal chairman and founder, George Jordan.

He stretched to get the kink out of his neck, recalling how proud George had been when he'd gifted the desk to Mark in celebration of his promotion to CEO eighteen months ago.

Since its founding in 1995, Dominal Industries had been a powerhouse, pioneering and manufacturing components required for health management machines, such as insulin pumps and blood pressure monitors. For more than twenty years, the Jordan family had held tight reins on the business, innovating both its product and business model to continue its domination of the market. Mark was the first leadership hire outside the Jordan family and was brought in to help George retire and sell the company.

Mark turned back toward the window. He had spent the better part of the afternoon going through the latest financial projections with Allan Chang, the chief financial officer for Dominal Industries, and reviewing the reports again by himself.

The news was not good.

Mark's office phone began to ring—once, twice, three times—but he stood perfectly still, focused on his breathing, and continued to stare out the window. A few moments later, there was a soft knock at the office door. His assistant peeked in. "Mark, it's Renata Campbell for you."

Renata Campbell, the managing partner for Gold Private Equity, had orchestrated the deal for Gold to buy Dominal Industries.

"Thanks. Please put her through." Mark moved slowly back toward his desk and sat down in his Herman Miller chair. He inhaled deeply and picked up the phone. "Hello, Renata. How are you?"

"Hi, Mark. I'm fine, thanks for asking." There was a slight echo as Renata was on speakerphone. "Hey, I know you're busy, but I need a few minutes of your time."

"Of course." Mark rubbed his forehead, preparing for the worst.

"I'm calling about the upcoming board meeting. I just want to give you a little insight on the internal discussions the investors are having."

Mark knew what was coming. He pictured Renata standing at her lightly stained maple desk, smoothing her straight black hair in the Wacker Drive high-rise office building that Gold occupied. He braced himself.

"Look, I know you've seen the numbers. The investors are going nuts. To put it bluntly, they're shitting their pants."

Mark's shoulders tensed. "Yeah, we're going through the details here. I know it looks bad, but I'm on it—"

"Mark," Renata said, cutting him off, "you've got to drive real results to turn this around. This has to be the best damn plan the board has ever seen, and you need to make sure you execute it flawlessly."

"I get it. There are definitely some additional cuts we can make to help profitability in the short term to show immediate impact."

"That's not enough. You need to be more deliberate and thoughtful in your actions to regain the board's confidence.

They're concerned that your team isn't focused on the right things."

Mark rose from his chair. "What do you mean?"

"Your sales strategy is unclear, operations seem inefficient, turnover is abysmal, and you still haven't hired a head of R&D yet. For God's sake, it's been twelve months!"

"I know. We've been out recruiting, but it's a tough market." Mark began pacing as far as his phone cord would allow.

"C'mon, Mark, you know that won't stand up. Xtele is making huge inroads into the market with cheaper versions of our products while probably building the next big thing, and you're blaming a tough recruiting market? Really?"

Mark ran his fingers through his wavy brown hair, which had just started graying at the temples—the only physical indication that he'd turned fifty earlier this year. Again, he stared out the big window.

"Look, you know I believe in you. I was the one who pushed the investors hard to promote you to CEO, remember? I convinced the other board members that you were ready to deliver the high performance that we needed, even though you had been the COO for such a short time. I also fought hard for you when you barely missed last year's targets."

Mark picked up his Boston Red Sox stress ball and rolled his eyes, having heard this reminder many times before. "Okay, what do I have to do to gain the rest of the board's confidence?"

"Get your leadership team focused, and do it now. This first quarter was a total disaster, and it's only going to get worse. You gotta fix this. This is your last chance. Do you understand?"

"Yes, I do. I assure you." Mark mustered all the confidence he could. "I promise, we'll demonstrate how we're going to turn this around at the next board meeting."

Mark hung up the phone, dropped back into his chair, and planted his head face down on the desk. A faint, dull roar could be heard from the adjacent building where machines churned out Dominal's product twenty-four hours a day. He suddenly felt nauseated.

The leadership team Mark had carefully built over the past eighteen months were all hard-working, committed professionals. Though they hadn't quite found their rhythm as a team yet, all the essential components were there. Some of the new leadership team members had left steady, good-paying jobs to take a chance with Dominal.

Then there were the 2,500 employees, some with more than twenty years of service. Their lives would be totally disrupted if Dominal had to be sold at a loss or started to lay people off.

Mark thought about his wife, Leanne, and their three kids. A lump rose in his throat. They'd never complained about having to sell their perfect Greystone home after he left Davis & Edwards and decided to take some time off. Leanne had stepped up in so many ways.

Mark cleared his throat and straightened up in his chair. He once again inhaled, held, and then exhaled. Suddenly, a flood of fresh ideas began to fill his head. He started typing like a madman.

A brief, loud knock interrupted Mark's flow.

Jen Schmidt, Dominal's chief human resources officer, opened the door and stepped in. "Hey, Mark. Do you have a minute?"

Mark nodded but continued staring at his monitor. Jen closed the door behind her and made her way over to the far end of his desk. She crossed her arms and stood for a moment, apparently hoping he would make eye contact.

"I wanted to let you know we just settled the Palmer case. He signed the severance agreement without incident. He accepted our first offer, which never happens. We're quite pleased with the outcome, and I thought you'd want to know." Jen gave Mark a satisfied smile.

"Uh, thanks, Jen," Mark murmured without removing his eyes from the screen.

Jen subtly cleared her throat. He didn't respond, trying to make it clear she was not going to get any further reaction from him on this issue. Just as she started to make her way to the door, Renata's words about the open positions echoed in Mark's head.

He snapped his head away from the monitor. "Hey, Jen, hold up a sec. How's the R&D search?"

Jen turned around from the middle of Mark's office, surprised. "We just discussed this in our last check-in. The team has been pounding the pavement."

"Okay, but do we have any new candidates?"

"No, we don't." Jen sighed and tilted her head. "It's a very tough market. We're doing everything we can."

"Are we, Jen? Are we really doing *everything* we can? It's been twelve months!" Mark blinked hard, feeling the pressure build up behind his eyes.

Jen took a few steps toward Mark's desk. "I've kept you in the loop the whole time. What more do you think we could be doing?"

"I don't know. Our competitors are out in the market building the next big thing—meanwhile, we can't even get one decent candidate in the door!"

"Mark, to be fair, you cut ten percent of our budget last year. I think I'm doing a pretty good job of doing more with less. I'm not sure what else we can do."

"You need to come up with something!" Mark shot up from his chair. "It's your job to get this role filled."

"Okay, then." Jen's hazel eyes looked past Mark at the steady drizzle outside of his office window. She straightened her tan suit. "Well, let me think through some options and get back to you."

"Wait, hang on." Mark held his hand up and slumped back into his chair. He motioned for her to sit down. He closed his eyes and rubbed his forehead. "You know, Jen, I just never thought we'd be here. We were at the top of our game when George sold eighteen months ago . . . and then, *boom*. Xtele just comes at us from out of nowhere. Now we're fighting to stay alive."

Jen shifted uncomfortably in her chair.

"Look, I've been meaning to talk to you." Mark folded his hands on his desk. "You know I believe in you, and you've done some really good work over the past year—including coaching me and other leaders through some difficult conversations and employee issues. Everyone at Dominal feels that you're approachable. We all feel you have a lot of potential . . ."

Jen sat perfectly still, staring at the beige carpet.

"I know we've asked you to do more with less, and you never push back. But lately, it feels like you're not focused on the right things. I think you need help rethinking your approach."

Jen's head jolted up. "I'm not sure I understand."

"Well, you know how you always talk about coaches for our high-potential leaders who just need some guidance, right?"

Jen nodded.

"Well, now it's your turn. I just learned about this consultant named Meg Beecham. She comes highly recommended from many people I trust in my network. She has a totally different approach to HR. Give her a business problem, and she develops a people solution. That's what you need." Mark handed Jen a business card.

"Okay." Jen accepted the card with a bemused look.

"I haven't had a chance to talk to her. Just make an appointment with her this week."

"With all due respect," Jen began, seeming to snap out of her trance, "I've got years of experience, and it's not like I'm new to Dominal."

"Yes, you're right. And your experience has been invaluable to us in many ways. I also believe you are the right person to lead HR long term, but we're stuck right now. The board is all over us about turnover and key positions going unfilled for too long. It's killing us. We need a fresh perspective if we're going to stay alive. These are HR challenges—*your* challenges—and I think you could use some help taking a different approach."

Jen sighed. "It doesn't sound like I have a choice."

"Well, the reality is we have to start thinking differently if we're going to get ahead of Xtele. We need to get these problems under control, and fast. Meg can help."

CHAPTER 2

MEG BEECHAM STOOD in the hallway across from the hotel ball-room, adjusting the satchel bag on her shoulder. She smoothed her black jeans and pulled at the cuffs of her white blouse, which were accented with little embroidered sunflowers. She sighed and started to plod her way toward the hotel bar, exhausted from her talk.

She turned right, passing through a charming hallway lined with small, inviting conference rooms. This old hotel, which stood in the heart of Chicago, was one of her all-time favorites. She'd been thrilled when the conference sponsors chose such a unique location. The hotel retained so much of its original look and feel—a timeless feel that she absolutely loved.

At precisely three in the afternoon, Meg arrived at the entrance of the nearly empty hotel bar. She loved this watering hole right in the middle of the hotel's historic lobby. The dimly lit room with a long, oversized oak bar from 1910 was the perfect place to take in a few craft beers and contemplate the bigger questions of life. It reminded her of the old pubs she'd frequented on her last trip to the English countryside.

The grand fireplace on the back wall spewed roaring flames, a perfect invitation to warm up at the end of a long autumn day. Out of the corner of her eye, Meg saw a woman sitting at a table near the back. Mid-thirties, shoulder-length brown hair, wearing a tailored black pantsuit, cream silk blouse, and black stilettos. The woman's eyes were scanning the room anxiously. Meg figured this must be her prospective client.

"Hi . . . Jennifer?"

The woman stood up, looking slightly confused at the casually dressed woman in front of her. She reached out her hand. "Uh . . . yes . . . Meg? Please, call me Jen. Thanks for making time for me."

Even though Meg's black boots gave her two extra inches, Jen was still quite a bit taller than her.

"No worries, Jen it is. I'm glad we were able to make this work." She put her bag down on the empty chair between them. "I actually just finished my talk a few minutes ago," Meg went on, taking a seat in the three-legged antique chair across from Jen.

"How did it go?"

Meg shrugged and gave a tired smile. "I think it went okay. Hard to tell." She picked up the small, laminated bar menu and studied it for a few seconds, then abruptly put it down, inclined her head slightly, and looked Jen straight in the eyes. "I know we just met, but can I ask you a favor?"

Jen blinked and jerked her head back. "Uh, sure, I guess."

"So, I'm not the best at giving these keynotes. I mean, I practice hard, but it still just takes it out of me. So, right now, I am *totally* spent. Could you please be patient with me today, you know, if I'm a little slow?"

"Not a problem." Jen chuckled. "I'm a working mother of two kids under six. I'm always running near empty. I completely understand."

Meg smiled. "I appreciate it." She tried to decide whether Jen matched the image in her head but was interrupted by the waiter.

"What can I get you two to drink today?"

"I'll take a Daisy Cutter Pale Ale, please. Jen, how about you?"

"Well, uh, I don't usually start drinking at three . . . but if you're having a beer, I guess I'll have a glass of the house white wine. Thank you."

"Love that you're willing to bend the rules," Meg exclaimed.

Jen smiled weakly. "When did you arrive in Chicago, Meg?"

"I actually came in over the weekend and took in a game at Wrigley Field."

Jen perked up. "Are you a baseball fan?"

The waiter arrived back at the table and quietly served their drinks.

"Not really. Back in LA, I have this friend who's a big Cubs fan . . . always going on about how great they are. I figured the least I could do was go to a game while I was here."

"I'm a huge Cubs fan, myself. Still get goosebumps when I think about the 2016 World Series. Sometimes my husband Dave and I rewatch Game 7 just to relive the magic."

"To the Cubs." Meg raised her mug to Jen. "My friend does the same thing and still tears up at the end. Who knew there could be so much history from a goat? What a game! I mean, how they came back from that rain delay . . . yeah, that was pretty cool."

Meg lifted her beer to eye level as she spoke, studying its color more closely. "It's a shame we don't get this beer at home." She took a satisfying slurp. "Well, here's to the next 108 or so years! Hopefully you don't have to wait that long again!"

"I'll drink to that!" Jen laughed and took her first sip of wine. "And I hope we have another successful postseason. You know, it's starting soon!"

Meg pulled up the sleeves of her blouse. "So, why do you think your boss asked you to reach out to me?"

"I'm not really sure. He just says he wants a different . . ." Jen's eyes grew large, and she stared at Meg's left wrist. "Sorry, I don't mean to be rude, but is that a tattoo?"

"Oh, yeah." Meg's blue eyes glanced down at her wrist. "It's Japanese kanji. Reminds me to be creative every day in order to be my best self."

"That's so cool!" Jen leaned over Meg's arm like a curious child. "What's your main creative outlet?"

"I write poetry," Meg replied. "I'm not published or anything … it's just a hobby. What about you? Do you have free time?"

"Very little," Jen admitted. "But I do love to paint. I've been drawing and painting my whole life. Not as much lately, though. I miss it."

"Any special type of painting?"

"Yes, I'm all about oil painting." Jen's hazel eyes brightened. "I love to take everyday sights and change the perspective of them through unique angles, colors, and shadows. It takes some thought and practice, but I find it really stimulating."

"Good for you. I find artistic people look at situations from different perspectives and typically offer more creative solutions."

"Interesting. I hadn't really thought about it that way." Jen took a sip of her wine.

"How's your wine?"

"Actually, not bad for a house. I think it's a sauvignon blanc." Jen glanced around the room. "This place is pretty cool. I've never been here before. My husband, Dave, would love it."

"Yeah, it's one of my favorite places in Chicago. A hidden gem." Meg felt a foam mustache forming on her upper lip and wiped her mouth with her napkin. "Great craft beer selection."

"Dave loves beer of all types, but when we go out, he likes to try different craft beers. I'm sure he'll want to come here for our next date night." Jen rolled her eyes. "So much for romance."

Meg laughed. "What does Dave do?"

"He's a finance director for an engineering firm. I give him a hard time about it, of course, but he's a great guy. He's been taking care of the kids a lot lately while I've been focused on work." Jen sipped her wine. "What about you? Married?"

"Not anymore," Meg said. "It was great while it lasted, but I think I'm just one of those people who does better alone."

"Marriage certainly isn't for everyone," Jen said softly, "but good for you for realizing what works best for your life."

"Thanks. Not many people understand."

Jen nodded, and they were both silent for a few moments.

"So, how did you end up at Dominal Industries?" Meg asked.

"Well, I worked with Allan, our CFO, early in my career at this company called Leal & Franklin. It was a professional services firm." Jen sipped her drink. "He was the finance manager back then. We stayed friends after we left, and he introduced me to Dominal shortly after it got sold to Gold."

"A strong relationship with the CFO is key." Meg acknowledged. "Tell me more about your background."

She listened intently as Jen traced her background, from graduating at the top of her class at the University of Illinois at Urbana–Champaign to taking on progressive roles in recruiting and HR in a variety of different industries—financial services, professional services, and tech.

"Your background is impressive. You've had some pretty significant roles, and it sounds like you've made a difference at every company."

"Thanks. I've worked hard, but also believe some of it was being in the right place at the right time."

"So, tell me a little more about what Dominal is facing now?"

"Well, we've recently been hit by a Chinese competitor that is quickly gaining market share." Jen pushed back a few strands of her brown hair that were in her face. "Our first-quarter financial performance was terrible, and our full-year projections don't look so great either. My boss, Mark, who's also the CEO, is pretty stressed out. It sounds like our board is all over him."

"I bet, that's a tough spot. What's your HR team like?"

"We have a good team—about ten people, including recruiters. We had to make cuts last year, but we've managed to make it work." Jen played with the damp cocktail napkin upon which her wine glass was resting. "So, maybe you could tell me a little about your background, Meg?"

"Sure. Well, I have over twenty-five years of experience. I started my career in IT and then took on roles in finance, strategy, and HR. I've had a few executive roles at a national bank and was a global talent executive at a Fortune 500 before starting my own company."

"Wow!" Jen exclaimed. "That's great—and pretty unique. I'm not sure I've ever met a finance person who can write poetry."

"You probably have, they just won't admit to it." Meg smirked. "People's talents are surprising when they let you see them."

"And what does your company do, exactly?" Jen sipped her wine slowly.

"Well, it's just me, and I left the corporate world to pursue this passion I have for helping companies think differently about HR—you know, move it away from its focus on compliance. I believe it's time to modernize the way HR functions, driving more growth and creating a place where people love to work." Meg straightened up in her chair. "So, I mostly advise CEOs on people strategies and programs to help them get there. Think of me as a fractional chief people officer."

"Interesting. But what if a company already has a chief people officer?" Jen sat up a bit and folded her hands in her lap.

"Don't worry, I'm not here to compete or take anyone's job. I promise. I'm here to add value. From time to time, I work with HR professionals, too, if that makes sense."

"So, you work alongside them?" Jen surmised.

"Yes, or end up translating between HR and the CEO, who aren't always aligned. I help get everyone on the same page."

"Do you focus on any specific industries or company size?"

"I'm industry agnostic—anything and everything from manufacturing to Bay Area tech startups. I do tend to focus on middle-market and emerging-growth organizations—a lot of investor-backed companies."

"Interesting." Jen rolled back her shoulders. "Like us. So, tell me more about how you work with clients?"

"What do you mean?"

"Well, do you have a process or methodology or program you follow?"

"Not really." Meg folded the edge of her cocktail napkin. "I mean, you know from your experience that every business is unique."

"True," Jen acknowledged. "But surely you have a standard approach?"

"I guess my approach is to understand the business challenges and then figure out the gaps. From there, I come up with a people solution. That's the only way you can drive better outcomes."

"Hmm . . ." Jen wore a puzzled expression. "Do you have an example?"

"I recently had a client who'd missed their operating targets for a few years. When we dug into it, their performance management system seemed disconnected from their business goals. Each year, over eighty-five percent of their employees were getting a 'meets expectations' or higher, even though the entire company was missing its operating targets. I helped them redesign their approach. This past year, their performance management results matched their business results, and, more importantly, they hit their goals."

"Yeah." Jen exhaled deeply. "We face a similar challenge. It's on my list to tackle eventually, but I'm not sure I've ever looked at things that way."

"Yes, it does take a different kind of thinking." Meg took a swig of beer. "But that's usually why I'm brought in."

"Well, that's intriguing. But I just don't know that I agree with Mark that this is the best way for me to be spending my time given current pressures."

"Hmm." Meg tilted her head. "What do you think would be a better use of your time?"

"I'm not sure." Jen sighed. "It's not you, Meg, it's just that I feel like I should be able to do what Mark is asking. I have years of HR experience. It's not like I'm new to the job."

"It's not a sign of weakness to bring in help." Meg swirled the remaining beer in her glass. "As a matter of fact, it's really a sign of strength. We all hit roadblocks no matter how much experience we have, right? And often a little help or a different perspective is what enables us to move forward."

"Yeah, I guess you're right."

Meg finished the last of her beer and put the glass down with a slight thud. "Look, I think I can help you and your team get focused on the key things you need to do to enable business growth."

Jen cast her eyes around the crowd gathering at the bar. The room had started to get noisy, and it was becoming hard for them to hear each other. A small group of conference attendees waved at Meg when they walked past their table. Jen studied Meg's expression when she waved back.

"Can I just say, you look exhausted."

"Ha, thanks, kind of you to notice." Meg nodded. "I *do* need some sleep—maybe on the flight home tomorrow—but I would like to continue this conversation. I'd love the opportunity to help."

"Okay." Jen swallowed her last sip of wine. "But I gotta warn you, between work and family, there's not a lot of extra time. I'll try my best."

"I understand. We'll do the best we can with the hours you have. I'd never want you to miss family time. That's not something you can ever get back."

"I appreciate that."

"One last thought before you go: I do things a bit differently. I hope that's okay."

"You don't say?" Jen cocked her head and smiled. "The finance–poetry combo was a dead giveaway."

"Yeah." Meg chuckled. "After I left corporate, I shed a lot of layers, but it's made me better at what I do. Have you ever heard of the movie *The Karate Kid*?"

"From the '80s? Yeah, I think I saw it when I was a kid."

"Likely. It's a classic, right? I loved it but forgot about it for years. Then, when I went out on my own, something brought me back to it. I ask every client to watch it. Are you open to this? I warned you I do things a bit differently."

"Ha. Sure, I guess."

"Great," Meg replied, smiling. "You can find it on one of the streaming services. Let me know when you've watched it, and we'll find a time to get started."

"Okay, sounds good." Jen gathered her purse.

Meg slung her satchel over her shoulder, shook Jen's hand, and the two women started walking toward the elevators. "Thanks again for coming out. I look forward to talking again soon. And thanks for understanding how tired I am. I was re-energized by our conversation."

"My pleasure," Jen said, stepping into the antique elevator that Meg knew headed toward the garage.

Directly across from her, Meg stepped into another elevator and headed up to her floor. She couldn't wait to order room service and hit the sack.

CHAPTER 3

JEN'S CELL BUZZED wildly on the particle board desk in her windowless office while she held her landline to her ear, waiting for Shauna to answer. She quickly picked it up and saw a string of text messages from Mark. It was only nine a.m., and she had already taken a few calming breaths given the craziness of the morning. Jen needed her head of HR operations, and *fast*. She tapped her pen on the desk rapidly while she waited.

Her cell phone buzzed again. She sighed, seeing it was a text from Allan: *Are you on your way? Mark's anxious.*

Jen texted back a thumbs-up emoji, hopeful that her long-time friend could placate Mark until she could get to the meeting. She closed her eyes and said a silent prayer that Shauna would pick up her phone soon.

Then, at last, Shauna picked up. "This is Shauna."

"Shauna, finally! Hey, remember what happened the last time there was an accident at the facility?"

Jen's cell buzzed again.

"Crap, Mark and Allan keep texting. I'm totally late for our leadership meeting. Anyway, remember how benefits misfiled the paperwork, and it cost the company a ton of money?" Jen played with the Wrigley Field paperweight on her desk while she listened to Shauna's response. "That's right, Shauna. Perfect. Yes, I need you on this immediately. Promise me you won't let history repeat itself, okay? Thanks. Gotta run."

Jen hung up the landline, grabbed her cell phone and a folder full of papers, and sprinted in her stilettos down the long, narrow hallway that showcased every award Dominal had ever won. She made her way past Mark's and Allan's offices, took a sharp right at the end of the hallway, and rushed into the board room just as Allan was presenting his department's latest projections. She stumbled slightly as she neared her place at the twenty-foot white marble conference table that dominated the rarely used formal meeting room that George Jordan had insisted on during the last office remodel. Allan picked up the papers that had slid out of Jen's folder and onto the beige carpet. He gave Jen a reassuring look when he handed them back to her.

"Ah, Jen, late as usual!" Rich Peters, Dominal's head of sales, interrupted as Jen regained her balance.

Mark shot Rich a stern look. "Everything okay, Jen?"

She adjusted her gray suit blazer. The large windows in the boardroom let in the bright, fall morning sunlight. Jen squinted a bit as she sat down.

"Yes. Sorry I'm late." Jen smiled insincerely at Rich. "There was an accident in the facility, and one of the supervisors was taken to the hospital. I was on the phone making sure benefits prepares the paperwork correctly this time." She turned to Mark. "That's why I couldn't pick up your call. I just didn't want to repeat that costly mistake we made last year."

"What's the name of the supervisor who was hurt?" Mark wore a concerned expression. "Is he okay? What happened?"

"Peter Morrill. Um, he's a . . ." Jen flipped through her papers. "Well, uh, I don't have a lot of details about his condition yet. I believe he was stable and alert when the ambulance left." Jen noticed everyone exchanging perplexed looks.

Allan leaned forward in his chair as though he was about to say something, when Michelle Johnson, Dominal's chief operations officer, jumped in.

"Peter is one of our shift supervisors. He's going to be fine. Apparently, there was an issue with the new honing machine, and he fell while evaluating the problem. Thankfully, Jerry was right there when it happened and reacted quickly to keep everyone calm and follow our safety procedures. I called his wife and plan to stop by the hospital on my way home."

Jen gave Michelle a quick smile, grateful for her support. They were hired around the same time and got along well both professionally and personally. They enjoyed an occasional drink after work to discuss the ins and outs of juggling motherhood, work, husbands, and the Cubs.

"Thanks, Michelle." Mark tapped his pen on the table. "Could you also give me his wife's number? I want to call after the meeting and offer my personal support to the family. I will also stop by the facility after this meeting and thank Jerry personally."

"That would be great. I know his wife would appreciate it. She was a bit nervous when I talked to her. I can't imagine getting a phone call like that." Michelle sighed. "But even she was relieved when I told her that Jerry was right there. I gotta tell you, I've worked with a lot of ops guys in my twenty years, and Jerry is by far the best director of logistics I've had the pleasure of meeting. We're really lucky to have him."

"For sure," Jen added. "I'll send flowers on behalf of Dominal."

Everyone seemed to contemplate Peter's predicament quietly for a few moments.

Mark broke the silence. "Okay, please keep us posted on Peter. Let's get back to it for now. Allan, can you please pick up where you left off?"

Allan returned to presenting projections and explaining how his team was partnering with sales and operations to improve performance.

"Allan, I assume your projections include the reductions we made last year in HR?" Jen pointed to the numbers on the page. "Those were pretty substantial, but we're committed to doing our part, even if it means we have to run lean."

Allan gave Jen a friendly nod. "It's all there."

Rich shared the progress of the new sales channels his team had identified and how he was driving performance across the sales territories. He once again highlighted the pricing pressure he was getting from Xtele.

"Hey, Rich, can we go back for a minute?" Jen asked after Rich had finished. "How are you coaching—"

"Our competitors are giving big discounts," Rich went on, cutting Jen off completely, "and I think that's where we're getting killed right now."

There was an uncomfortable silence in the grand room for a few moments. Jen and Michelle exchanged knowing glances. Allan shifted uneasily in his chair. Everyone was on edge awaiting Mark's response.

"We're not known as the cheapest provider." Mark pursed his lips. "We're the quality play. That's one thing that differentiates us. We're not sacrificing margins."

"I know," Rich argued, "but it's hard to compete when Xtele is selling so cheap, and everyone else is discounting twenty percent on already lower prices. We've got to stay competitive."

"Damn it, Rich—you know Gold will never go for discounts! We may as well pack up our stuff now if that's all we've got." Mark slammed the table with both hands.

Michelle stood up as she presented several operational improvements she was in the process of implementing, explaining how they would improve efficiency by twenty-five percent.

"We need to be completely sure of those numbers." Mark looked at Michelle and then Allan. "If we're off, the board's going to be up our ass!"

"Agreed." Michelle started to walk laps around the long boardroom table at a head-turning pace.

"Really, Michelle?" Allan's eyes got wide. "You're like the Energizer Bunny!"

"You know I can't sit still!" Michelle exclaimed. "We ops folks gotta walk the floor."

"If you say so." Allan shook his head and shifted his focus back to the group. "Look, everyone, Michelle and I are scheduled to go through the numbers again to explore more opportunities later today."

Everyone in the room seemed energized and ready to execute their action plans. Mark adjusted the collar of his light gray dress shirt and smiled slightly. He turned to his head of HR.

"Okay, Jen, you're up."

Jen passed her presentation handouts to everyone in the room. The team rustled through the pages.

Jen cleared her throat. "The good news is that our time to fill open positions is down, so we're hiring faster. As you can see, turnover is steady. We've reached out to ten more candidates for the R&D director role this quarter, so we're still pounding the pavement on that search. We've held down our HR operating costs from last year's cut, and our employee claims and injuries are also down. All in all, I'd say we're headed in the right direction . . ."

Sensing a subtle change in the room's energy, Jen paused and glanced up from her handout. Everyone had their faces buried in her printouts, and she couldn't read their expressions as usual.

"Okay, let's continue with an update on benefits: We're finishing open enrollment prep. More good news—our benefit carriers are only raising prices two percent compared to the standard five percent. Allan and I thought it'd be a great idea to split the two percent between the employees and Dominal to show we're all in this together while also helping profitability." Jen glanced at Allan.

Mark looked at Allan to gauge his response. Allan gave a small nod to Jen and then focused back on his handouts, apparently avoiding Mark's gaze.

"Finally, on the last slide"—Jen flipped the page—"I'd like to talk about our cultural initiatives. We have a company-wide survey launching next month, which should help give us some insight into turnover."

"Thank you, Jen." Mark glanced around the room. "Anyone have any questions or feedback?"

No one made eye contact with Mark or Jen. The lack of interest was palpable. Jen felt defeated and wondered why the leadership team was showing such apathy for a key area like HR.

"Way to push the paper forward," Rich said sarcastically while turning his head to Jen. "As usual, we're all on the edge of our seats with the HR update."

"Knock it off, Rich," Mark snapped. "If you have constructive feedback, be professional and share it."

"Nothing to add." Rich sulked. "Sorry."

"Okay, thanks everyone." Mark wrapped up the meeting. "We're getting there, but there's still a ton of work to do. Let's meet again tomorrow."

"Thanks for making the time to meet with me, Mark."

"My pleasure, Meg. Give me one second." The intense, late afternoon sun was causing a glare on his Zoom call, so he adjusted his screen to see Meg clearly.

"No problem." Meg sat in her home office with the unusual, gentle pitter-patter of Los Angeles rain hitting the windows. "It's nice to be face-to-face, albeit over video. Were my initial comments on Jen's deck helpful?"

"Yes, very much so. Appreciate you sending those over."

"Sure. What else can I do to help?"

"Well . . ." Mark wrung his hands. "Like I said in my email, we're in the fight of our life. We just did a first review of board presentations, and the sales, ops, and finance plans are making progress, but I'm worried we're going to get creamed on HR."

"I've worked with companies backed by Gold in the past," Meg said slowly. "They're intense. You're really going to have to be crisp and buttoned-up."

"Yeah, exactly!" Mark's eyes were wide. "But you saw Jen's slides. You know the board couldn't care less about any of that right now. We're bleeding people!"

"You need specific actions."

"Yes, we need actions!" Mark sat back in his chair. "Real, hard-hitting actions! Not crap and spin and future surveys! Ugh, sorry, Meg, I don't mean to lose my cool."

"No worries, I get it." Meg smoothed her favorite black-and-white sweater with a hint of silver thread. She always felt these small embellishments brought her personality into a professional setting without being over the top. "Did you give Jen feedback?"

"I didn't." Mark glanced out the window. "And yes, I know I need to . . . she deserves at least that. But I'm struggling with what to tell her. Jesus, I'm doing a crappy job leading her."

"Hey, go easy on yourself." Meg tucked her short, blonde hair behind her ears. "What you are going through is tough, really tough. And even in normal circumstances, no CEO can solve every problem for every person on his leadership team. Part of being a good leader is acknowledging when someone needs support that you can't provide."

"Yeah, to be honest, Meg . . ." Mark cast his eyes toward the ceiling. "I feel like I've let the team down. I'm usually so good at spotting trends. Hell, it led to the end of my career at Davis & Edwards because I was so adamant about what I believed would happen. How did I miss Xtele?"

"No one can predict every trend." Meg noticed a large puddle forming outside the French door of her office. She looked back at Mark. "How long have you been CEO?"

"About eighteen months." Mark rubbed his eyes. "Took over from the founder when we sold to Gold."

"Is this your first CEO job?"

"Yeah, before this, I was the chief strategy officer at Davis & Edwards for years. I saw the market fundamentally shifting and couldn't get anyone to agree that we needed to change our business model. They ended up asking me to leave."

"I've heard the story," Meg acknowledged. "I'm sure that was hard. Especially because you were right in the end."

"Yeah, I knew the challenges would be different as CEO, so I've really been focused on building the team." Mark looked away from the screen and put his head in his hands. "You know, maybe I just took my eye off the ball."

"Or maybe this wasn't something you could have seen coming." Meg tried to make eye contact with Mark. "Look, there's no point in dwelling on the past—you're focused now on mitigating this threat, right?"

"Yeah, but I am still struggling with Jen." Mark shook his head. "You know, I really strive to be a servant leader, but . . . right now, I feel like I just don't have it in me. I need her to step up."

"Okay, Mark—first, we're having this conversation on the best way to help her, so that's exactly how you're guiding her," Meg said. "And second, you have to figure out the best use of your time. Dwelling on this situation with Jen is only using up your energy when you should be focused on getting ready for this meeting with Gold."

"You're right." Mark sat up in his chair. "Listen, do you have time to help Jen get this presentation ready?"

"I will make time. But it's up to you to talk to Jen about it. I can't force her to accept my help."

"Yeah." Mark adjusted his glasses. "Any thoughts on how I should approach it?"

"Well, maybe start from a place of curiosity. Ask her what she thought the board's reaction would be to what she presented."

Mark shook his head. "She'll most likely respond with, 'As usual, no engagement.' They never have anything to say."

"That's a problem, right? Given the issues you've highlighted." Meg took a sip of water. "I mean, you need the board to engage with what she presents."

"I do." Mark tapped his pen on the desk. "The problem is I don't think she's ever thought about it that way."

"Yeah, you're probably right," Meg agreed. "Her presentation is a tactical department summary when you need it to be a company growth action plan. Perhaps you can help her understand that leaders at this level are focused on the latter."

"That's good." Mark jotted down notes. "I may use that with all of my team."

"Look, the key to your approach is to be curious, not furious. Listen to what she has to say, and address it in a way that feels natural to you. You will guide her to the right answer."

"Ha!" Mark chuckled. "I love the 'be curious, not furious.' That's great. I'll give it a try."

———— ∽◦∾ ————

After lunch, Mark trudged down the hallway to Jen's office. He paused to look at his favorite award: Fastest Growing Company 2016. They'd earned it the year he'd joined the company. He smiled, remembering the excitement he and George had felt when they'd won and the fancy ceremony he and Leanne had attended to receive the award on behalf of Dominal.

Mark sighed and continued down the hall, reflecting on his conversation with Meg and trying to prepare himself for the discussion he was about to have with Jen.

Just outside her office, he stopped, looked down at his black dress shoes, inhaled, and held it. After slowly releasing his breath, he walked through the door. "Have a few minutes, Jen?"

"Yeah, hey, sure. Have a seat." Jen cleared the empty lunch containers from her desk and threw them in the trash. "What can I do for you?"

Mark sat down and glanced around Jen's office. Her tattered particle board desk was on its last legs and had probably been around since Dominal was founded. Clearly, she had tried to brighten the space with some colorful abstract art pieces that matched the hideous pieces in his office, but they felt out of place. On her credenza, Mark noticed the single picture of her family posing by the 2016 Cubs World Series Trophy. He made a mental note that she deserved better furniture once Dominal got itself out of its current predicament.

"So, I wanted to talk to you about your board presentation."

"Sure." Jen pulled out a pad of paper from a drawer in the rickety desk. "What's up?"

"Well, let me ask you, what did you think the board's reaction would be to what you presented today?"

"Umm . . ." Jen seemed to stall for time. "Well, I don't really know. For the most part, it's the usual presentation we give to the board, but I modified it to focus on how we were going to address the turnover issue and to provide more detail on the R&D search like you asked."

"And given the pressure we're under, how did you think they'd respond?"

"Sorry." Jen had a puzzled look. "I don't follow."

"Okay." Mark brushed a speck off his gray slacks. "Did you think they'd feel like we have it under control and can fix the problems based on what you presented?"

"Well, I guess. I thought that's what I covered in my slides." Jen sighed. "I mean, it's not like they really have a lot to say about HR."

"But don't they?" Mark argued. "I mean, they're all over us about turnover and open positions. Isn't that HR?"

"Yeah, I guess." Jen looked down. "But they never seem to want to talk about what I present."

"True." Mark angled his head to the side. "And part of that's my fault. I should've provided you with more guidance on how to engage them. So, let me try to start with that now. Look, what you presented today is a great tactical HR summary, but it's not a board presentation."

Jen shook her head. "I don't follow."

"There weren't enough tangible actions in your plan and too many check-the-box activities that aren't going to help us get out of our current situation. We need more hard-hitting actions from HR."

"Okay," Jen's eyes widened. "But this is what HR does. I want to help, but you have to give me more direction. I'm not a mind reader."

"Yes, and I'm not an HR person, and neither are our board members." Mark put a hand on each of the chair's armrests. "So, you need to think about this more as a company-level action plan. What are you going to do that is going to help Dominal solve its business problems? This is *your* area. You've got to figure out the right action steps, just like me and everyone else on the leadership team."

Jen looked down at her hands in her lap. Mark could sense her frustration.

"I know you and Shauna have been working hard on this, but this just isn't working. We need a new approach." Mark tried to get back to Meg's guidance—to be curious, not furious. "How did your meeting go with Meg Beecham?"

"We met last week when she was in town." Jen looked up. "She is clearly smart. I plan to work with her as I have time. She's just a bit . . . you know . . . different. Her first assignment was for me to watch *The Karate Kid* again. Anyway, Dave and I watched it—but I have no idea why. And now Dave's practicing all the karate moves he picked up, and it's driving me nuts!" Jen forced a thin smile.

Mark chuckled. "I remember that movie well. Ralph Macchio. Mr. Miyagi, right?" Jen nodded, and Mark was quiet for a few moments.

"Look, Jen," he said gently. "I took the liberty of reaching out to Meg to discuss your presentation today. I think the two of you should go through it as soon as possible. She had some good initial thoughts based on our short conversation."

Jen's head shot back. "Well, I was planning to work with her."

"Yeah, I know. Don't take it personally, I wasn't trying to go behind your back. I know I can't give you the guidance you need to solve this problem, but I can give you a resource. Meg is someone who can help you right now. We need her. You need her."

Jen's shoulders slumped. "Okay."

"Reach out to her and get on the phone with her first thing tomorrow. We need new ideas ASAP."

CHAPTER 4

AT NINE O'CLOCK the next morning, Jen sat at her desk and scarfed down a chocolate croissant. She brushed the crumbs off her desk and pulled out a notebook from the top drawer before connecting to the Zoom meeting that Meg had set up.

"Hi, Meg—sorry, just finishing breakfast," Jen mumbled while chewing. "Thanks for making the time. I know it's early in LA."

"No problem. This is important." Meg was sipping an enormous mug of coffee with "Not Crazy . . . *Creative*" written on the front. "I had a chance to review your presentation. Mark sent it over. I'd like to get your perspective."

"I don't get it. His feedback doesn't make sense. We're doing better on recruiting, holding steady on turnover, negotiating hard with our vendors, getting the engagement survey in place . . . should I go on?"

"Those are all positives. But let me ask you, what does Mark say are his top business goals right now?"

Jen processed Meg's question as she took a sip of coffee. "To get the business back on track and meet this year's aggressive growth targets, I believe."

"And what's stopping him from taking a people perspective?"

"Everything I mentioned—which is why I covered them all in my presentation." Jen put her hand to her forehead and rubbed at what felt like the beginning of a headache. "Sorry, Meg. It's not you. I'm just frustrated."

Meg smiled patiently. "I get that. This isn't easy. Let me ask you a few other questions just to get the lay of the land. What did everyone else present at the meeting?"

"Well, Allan laid out the financial projections and identified performance bottlenecks and some things he was going to do to get the business going again. Rich provided some actions to restart sales, and Michelle talked about improving operational efficiencies."

"And Mark's reaction?" Meg tapped on the coffee cup on her desk.

"He asked a lot of questions and gave good feedback. Honestly, Meg, I don't think he likes the people side of the business."

"Maybe you're right. But the fact that you and I are having this conversation tells me he thinks there is more to do on the people side."

"Okay, good point," Jen admitted, "but I still don't know *what* he wants."

"One more question—the other presentations, were these their usual board updates?" Meg picked up a metal Slinky Jr. from her desk and bounced it back and forth.

"No, not really. I mean, they did present the usual performance summary slides, but the other slides were different." Jen rubbed her forehead. "But my slides were different too. They weren't fluff, if that's what you're implying. Is that a Slinky?"

"Yep, it helps me think." Meg looked away from the monitor. It was early in LA, and Jen guessed Meg was watching the sunrise from her office window. "Your slides weren't fluff. But did you notice that everyone else's action plans were directly connected to the critical challenges the business is facing?"

"Well, it's easier for them because their areas are the problems right now," Jen argued.

"Perhaps. But let's take finance for a moment." Meg carefully placed her Slinky back on her desk and leaned forward. "Their job is to report the numbers and manage and allocate the financial resources, right? They aren't necessarily a direct problem area like sales and ops. Yet, you said Mark engaged with Allan's presentation, right?"

"Yes, but we're bleeding money right now. Of course, it's a direct problem area."

"Okay, but with your turnover issues, couldn't we make the same argument about the people side of the business?" Meg leaned even closer to the monitor. "Isn't it fair to say that you're bleeding *people* right now?"

Jen pulled back in her chair. She cocked her head and rubbed her temples. "I . . . I don't know. I mean, I've never looked at it that way."

"Listen, HR and finance have the same opportunity to influence business outcomes. One is responsible for allocating financial resources, the other human resources—and in today's economy, a company needs both."

"I guess that makes sense." Jen began to write some notes. "But I'm showing how we're allocating resources with metrics, like time-to-fill."

"Good. Let's dig into that. What does time-to-fill mean to someone like Mark?"

"It shows him how quickly we're filling open roles." Jen took another sip of her coffee.

"Sure, but how does that impact Mark and other company leaders? Let's say we're filling roles faster. What would that mean for Dominal?"

Jen shifted in her chair and thought for a moment. "Well, it would mean that we're improving our efficiency and, I guess, our bottom line."

"Okay, but time-to-fill is HR jargon, isn't it? In my career, I've fallen flat on my face using these types of terms. They don't mean anything to business leaders. Yes, it's important to measure the efficiency of your recruiters, but you need to put this in a business context for people outside of HR. What is the business impact of not filling a role?"

"Okay . . . I'm really trying to follow you, but I'm not sure I . . ."

"Let me give you an example. Years ago, I worked in professional services. We communicated the days a job was open in terms of missed revenue opportunities and impacts to client service because these were the business goals of the organization. This helped our executives understand much better how recruiting was performing versus the time-to-fill metric."

"But Dominal is manufacturing, not services," Jen corrected.

"But you get the connection, don't you?" Meg rested her chin on her hands. "Let's think about it another way. What is the impact of having open sales roles at Dominal?"

"Hmm . . . well, I guess sales productivity would be impacted."

"And would revenue be impacted? If you don't have a full sales team, can it fill its lead pipeline and grow existing relationships?"

"No, I guess not." Jen fiddled with her pen under her desk. "So, I should be talking about open sales roles in terms of missed revenue opportunities? That would be totally different. But what about operations roles?"

"Ask yourself the same question—what happens in the facility when there are open operations roles?"

"I suppose we can't do as much." Jen gently leaned her head back and stared at the ceiling for a moment. "Okay, I'm starting to see it. Maybe you have a point. I can tie my metrics more closely to the top and bottom line."

Meg smiled broadly. "So, let's talk about turnover. How long has it been this high?"

"Definitely since I got here eighteen months ago, and it sounds like it has been the norm for the last several years."

"And do you have any data around turnover? Exit interviews? Prior engagement surveys? Perhaps even Glassdoor reviews?" Meg picked up her Slinky again.

"Well . . ." Jen shifted and rubbed her head again. "Let me think. It's scattered in bits and pieces."

"The big issue I see is that turnover has been a problem for many years, and your solution is to implement something next month that will start the process of helping you diagnose why employees have been leaving Dominal at unacceptable rates for the past several years. Does that sound right?"

Meg stared into the computer screen and peered into Jen's eyes.

"Let's go back to finance for a minute," Meg continued. "Say the company had been running out of cash every month for several years. What if Allan came to the meeting and said that he was going to run an analysis a month from now that would help him start to understand why the company is running out of cash every month?"

"Well, of course we'd be out of business! When you put it that way, it sounds ridiculous!" Jen was horrified. "But I get what you're saying—we can't just say we're looking into it, we need to dig in and come up with some key themes on why people are leaving the organization before the board meeting."

"Great!" Meg sat back in her chair. "Why don't you develop some actions to address those?"

"I do have a theory about what's causing our high turnover. I know there is some feedback on Glassdoor about how our managers can be unprofessional. Maybe Shauna and I can think through some things we can do to change that."

Meg placed her Slinky back on her desk. "Good. Is this helping you?"

"Yes, I think it is. I mean, you're definitely raising some good points."

"Excellent. The key is to connect everything you are doing to the business. You need short-term actions to stop the bleeding and long-term strategies to address issues systemically. That's what will engage the board and give them confidence that you have a handle on these issues."

"Makes sense."

Meg glanced at the clock on the blue wall in her office. "We only have a few minutes left. My suggestion is that you focus on reducing turnover and your open roles. This is going to be hard; ninety-nine percent of what you come up with will not be relevant, but don't feel bad about that. Just like Daniel-san had to practice 'wax on, wax off' to learn his first karate move, you'll need to keep questioning yourself about every action you come up with: 'How is this helping Dominal achieve its business goals?' If you can't answer that question, it doesn't belong on the slides. Make sense?"

"Yeah, it does." Jen smiled. "I'll get with my HR operations leader and start brainstorming. Can I reach out if we get stuck?"

"Of course. I'm here to help. Text or call anytime. Remember, how does it help Dominal achieve its business goals? Be maniacal about it. Wax on, wax off!" Meg moved her hands in a circular motion.

Jen laughed and thanked Meg. She disconnected from the Zoom call and picked up her office phone to call Shauna so they could get right to work.

"No way. It won't work, Shauna." Jen shook her head frantically as she pushed her kung pao chicken around the takeout container with her chopsticks. "They will never go for it." She turned her head and stared out the conference room window into the dark fall night. "We have to think of something else."

Mark had excused Jen from the leadership team meeting so she could refocus her presentation. She and Shauna had cancelled all their afternoon meetings and locked themselves in the small HR conference room down the hall from Shauna's office. The room was far away from any high-traffic areas, which made it a coveted spot for small, focused meetings—despite its dated furniture, faded blue carpet, and peeling off-white paint.

But hours later, they were still stuck.

"Jen, we have no choice." Shauna sighed. "You know that no potential candidate is picking up the phone when we call. It's a senior-level search; we need to rethink our approach." She took the last bite of her Mongolian beef and rice and stood up to throw out the container.

Jen turned back to Shauna. "Right now, I just can't see spending that kind of money to bring in outside help. How would our team feel?"

Shauna slowly walked back to the table and brushed the fortune cookie crumbs off her gray cardigan sweater. She leaned forward on the faux wood conference table and looked Jen in the eyes. "Honestly? I think they'd be happy that we're finally taking the problem seriously."

"What?!"

"Don't get me wrong, Jen—no one wants to see us spend a bunch of money. But think about how disheartening it is to go after people day after day and get no response, and then be reminded regularly how disappointed the CEO is. We're simply not equipped to do this in house. Think about how much time we've wasted focusing our recruiters on this single search with all the other open roles we have to fill?"

Jen exhaled loudly and turned back to the window. Exhaustion was setting in. "Maybe you have a point."

"Really?" Shauna said excitedly. "Okay! So, now what? Should we quantify how much time we have spent on the search so far? You know . . . so the investment doesn't look out of sync with the goal?"

Jen continued to stare out the window. She rubbed her neck and shoulder before turning back to Shauna.

"No." She shook her head. "That's not going to tell us much, other than we've spent a lot of money already and have gotten nowhere. I think it goes back to what Meg said. We have to connect this action to Dominal's business goals." Jen perked up a bit. "Perhaps we try to quantify the impact on the business—you know, what it costs to *not* have an R&D leader. Meg told me that she'd successfully used a similar tactic, so maybe the same approach could work for us."

Shauna looked puzzled. "How would we even get started with that calculation?"

"That's a good question. I need to think about it and maybe discuss this with Allan tomorrow. For now, let's go with the retained search firm option."

"Sounds good," Shauna said.

"Let's sleep on all this, and I'll talk to Mark in the morning." Jen glanced down at her watch and looked over at Shauna. "Wow, look at the time! Thanks again for staying with me and for all your help. Sorry you had to cancel your date with Ravi."

Shauna smiled. "You're welcome. Don't worry, Ravi understands. I'm happy to help. I have to say, I feel like we just ran a marathon. I'm exhausted, yet exhilarated. This is cool!"

<hr/>

The next morning, before eight o'clock, Mark was sitting at his desk, reviewing the key messages of his board presentation, when he heard a knock at his office door.

"Good morning, Mark. Here are the turnover reports you asked for—HR just delivered them." His assistant handed him the reports.

"Thank you!" Mark called out as she left his office and closed the door.

He studied the summary. "Shit!" He threw the pages down on his desk, stood up, and walked across the room, staring out at the gray sky. The numbers were trending the wrong way. "So much for holding steady," he muttered.

An hour later, Jen appeared outside Mark's office doorway while he was wrapping up a call. He motioned for her to come in and sit down.

"Morning . . ." Mark hung up the phone. "Sorry I'm late. I just wanted to wish Jack luck on his school project. He was a bit nervous. So, I heard you and Shauna were burning the midnight oil last night."

"Yeah." Jen nodded. "I knew how important it was to get you something today."

"Good, because I just saw the latest turnover numbers." Mark shook his head and sighed. "Depressing. Let's take a look at what you have."

Jen handed her updated slides to Mark. "I met with Meg yesterday and reworked the slides with Shauna. I want to see if this is more in line with what you had in mind."

Mark took the handout from Jen and started flipping through the slides.

"We found that the majority of our turnover is coming from ops people reporting to five different supervisors," Jen explained. "Our first action is to coach those managers to see if we can at least stop the bleeding and perhaps also figure out what kind of management training they're going to need—but we also realized that we may be paying below market and not attracting the right caliber of talent. Meg suggested some analysis to see if we can adjust our compensation practices."

"You're suggesting we pay people more?" Mark's brown eyes widened.

"Not necessarily, but we need to analyze the situation and determine if raising compensation will attract talent that will stick, which would be more profitable overall."

"Hmm . . . okay, that's interesting. You will need to get with Allan, and we'll need to figure out the right messaging on this because the board will react negatively if we just say we're going to pay more. Do you think we should pull Meg into that discussion?"

"Yeah, I plan to work with Meg and Allan on how to position it to the board." Jen turned the page. "And then, on to the R&D search. I am recommending that we retain a search firm. I know it's a lot of money, but if we need to make the case, I can get with Allan to show the impact of not having the role filled."

"I don't think you will need to convince anyone of the impact of not filling the role. Renata was pretty clear about the board's feelings on this," Mark acknowledged. "Nice work, Jen. This feels like a good start. Let's run it by the leadership team this afternoon."

After her meeting with Mark, Jen grabbed her coat and walked to Dominal's front entrance. The cold fall breeze hit her face the moment she opened the door. She breathed it in and pulled up her coat collar. This was just what she needed. Making her way to the side of the building, she turned into an abandoned courtyard covered with beige rock that surrounded a dried-up reflecting pool. She settled onto one of the three stone benches and pulled out her phone to read through a few text messages from Dave about the kids. She smiled, put the phone back in her pocket, and stared across the back parking lot toward a small, wooded park. Lost in her thoughts, she closed her eyes and breathed in the crisp air.

"Is this seat taken, ma'am?"

"Michelle!" Jen was startled. "Sorry, I'm just getting some fresh air. Here, have a seat." She scooted over to make room for Michelle. "You out walking? How many steps so far?"

"I didn't mean to scare you." Michelle sat down. "Yeah, I relieved Jerry at five in the morning. We have a few people out sick, and he's been pulling too many double shifts. Anyway, my watch died after I hit 25,000 steps. So typical!"

Jen laughed. "You know you're the only person with that problem. I wish I could bottle your energy. I could've used it last night."

"I heard you and Shauna were here pretty late."

"Yeah," Jen replied, "but we got a lot done. I talked to Mark, and he seemed to like the plan."

"That's good to hear, Jen. You doing okay?"

"I think so," Jen exhaled. "It's just a lot. I know everyone's working hard, but . . . you know, I miss the kids, and I feel bad that Dave's doing everything right now."

Michelle pushed back her blonde hair against the wind. "I know. Me too. I can't remember the last time I had a conversation with Joe that wasn't about who was picking up the kids or where we were ordering takeout."

"I guess this is having it all, right?" Jen chuckled.

"Yeah, who knew it would be so great?" Michelle smiled.

"When things settle down, we are way overdue for a cocktail!"

"For sure."

Jen looked at her watch. "I guess we should head back in."

"Yep, back to the battle." Both women stood up and slowly walked back toward the main entrance. As they rounded the corner, they ran smack into Mark, who was walking briskly toward the front parking lot.

"Jen. Michelle. Hi. Where are you two coming from?"

"Just getting some fresh air." Jen shivered. "Took advantage of the courtyard to do some thinking."

"I go out there to clear my head sometimes too." Mark adjusted his gray wool scarf and nodded slowly. "I like to sit and listen to the low hum of the machines from the factory floor. It's comforting. Gives me the sense that things are still moving forward at Dominal, despite our challenges. Anyway, right now I'm out for a quick walk before our lunch meeting. We've been so busy, I haven't been able to work out, and I'm feeling a bit sluggish. Now, let me guess, you two were huddling in the courtyard to talk about the Cubs, right?"

"For once, Mark, we were actually *not* talking about the Cubs." Michelle gave a knowing smile to Jen. "I think that's a first for us."

"I don't believe it," Mark shook his head. "Surely, you're thinking about whom the Cubs might face postseason."

"Not yet," Michelle smiled, "But it's on our list to tackle right after the board meeting."

"Of course it is! I'll be doing the same thing for the Red Sox." Mark put his hands in his coat pockets. "If not the Cubs, what *was* the hot courtyard topic?"

"We were just thinking it's been a while since we had a happy hour. You should come next time, Mark." Jen shifted in her stilettos, wishing she had put on her sneakers before coming out. "We have a lot of fun complaining about our spouses and kids."

"I have three teenagers. I think my stories can beat yours, hands down." Mark rolled his eyes.

Michelle and Jen quietly giggled.

"Thank you both for everything you're doing. I know this feels really hard right now," Mark added softly, "but it won't always be like this. We just gotta win the board's confidence. I'll see you both back inside." Mark strode off waving as Jen and Michelle walked back into the warmth of the lobby.

Mark poured dressing on his grilled chicken salad while the rest of the leadership team grabbed plates and situated themselves at the long conference room table. The windows were dotted with fresh raindrops. Allan turned the can lights to full power to brighten the room before sitting down.

"This was the only time we had available today," Mark said to the group. "I hope the fact that we're serving food makes it a little better."

"You know you can bribe me with food anytime." Rich smiled. The rest of the team chuckled, easing the tension a bit.

"Let's get started. You know that Jen and her team spent all day yesterday reworking their action plan. I reviewed it this morning with her and want to get everyone's perspective." Mark turned to Jen. "Please, go ahead."

Jen wiped her fingers with her napkin. She passed out her slides and walked the leadership team through the key pieces of the action plan she shared with Mark earlier that day.

"Wow!" Michelle gasped as she looked at the data. "I knew these supervisors had challenges, but not to this extent! I can't believe so much of the turnover is connected to these five supervisors."

"Yeah, we have a whole set of actions related to helping these managers, as you can see. I've also noted that we should review the pay structure."

"Hmm . . ." Allan chimed in. "I'm not sure how that will land with the board right now."

"I don't know, Allan." Michelle stood up and walked to the trash can at the end of the boardroom to throw out her lunch container. "I think Jen has a point. We should think about how we want to pay operations folks long term. I know pay is an issue, and it's probably true that we don't have the right talent in some roles. What if we could reduce turnover significantly? If we want to produce the best quality products, we can't have subpar talent."

"We need a true pay philosophy, and maybe that's the way we pitch it to the board. We can say that we're investigating the connection between turnover and pay," Jen added. "What about the R&D search? Is everyone okay with us going external?"

"Totally. We should have done it months ago," Allan acknowledged. "We need to get this done—and I don't see any other way, given the slow progress."

"And we need our recruiters to focus on sales roles," Rich added. "I think one of my actions needs to be to have a full team in thirty days. Do you think that's possible, Jen?"

Jen rolled her shoulders back. "Yes, that's where I would redeploy the recruiters currently working on the R&D search."

"Well, hang on," Michelle chimed in from the corner. "It's clear from this that we also need some focus on the open operations roles. Everything can't go to Rich just because he runs sales."

"Let me remind you—there's no ops without sales, Michelle!" Rich interjected. He took another bite of his sandwich.

"I agree with you, Michelle," Jen responded, "but first I think the more important opportunity for ops is the turnover. Once we've stabilized just a bit, I can deploy more resources to ops too."

"I don't love it, but I understand it." Michelle sat back down and brushed the crumbs from her lunch off the table. "Jen, this is really good data. I'm planning on getting with Jerry and his team after this meeting, and I may pull in Shauna later this week if she has time to discuss the coaching piece."

"Thanks." Jen smiled at Michelle. "Let's get through the board meeting tomorrow, and then I'm sure she'll make time."

"Great work, everyone." Mark closed the lid of his empty salad container. "Jen, let's adjust the plan based on this discussion and continue to refine. Then everyone needs to get in the right mindset so we're ready to go for tomorrow afternoon's meetings. I don't need to remind you there's a lot on the line here."

CHAPTER 5

"OKAY, EVERYONE—SIXTY MINUTES until game time. How're we feeling?" Mark nervously tugged each of the sleeves of his dark blue shirt, then glanced around at the team of four gathered in his office. The afternoon sunlight streaming in from the windows brightened the room.

The leadership team had finalized the board materials earlier in the day and were doing one last check-in before the board meeting at three. Jen sat still at Mark's small conference table, studying each member of the team, awaiting their reactions.

"I feel like we've prepared for war." Allan tapped his papers on the table. "And I'm ready for the battle!"

"Seriously, Mr. Chang, you live for the battle." Mark shook his head. "Sorry, my friend, but you're not a good spokesperson for the team on this question."

"Fair enough." Allan winked.

"What about the rest of you?" Mark asked.

"It's a solid plan," Michelle added, tapping her foot underneath the table.

"Jeez, Michelle, you think you could sit still for a minute? The whole table is vibrating." Rich shook his head. "How are you going to make it through the board meeting?"

Michelle rolled her eyes at Rich.

"Look, it's not going to be an easy meeting," Rich acknowledged, "but I think we've done everything we can to prepare for wherever they go, boss."

"Yeah, this is totally different from anything we've done before." Jen smiled a bit nervously. "But it could just work."

Mark looked around at his leadership team and smiled. "Everyone has worked really hard, and I want to thank you for everything. This is our moment. Look, this is our World Series. Let's show them who's the champion, okay? I'll see you in the boardroom shortly."

The leadership team slowly gathered their stuff and made their way out of Mark's office. Jen was gathering the last of her papers when her cell buzzed. She felt her eyes go wide when she read the incoming text.

Mark caught Jen's expression. "Everything okay, Jen?"

"Um, yeah, everything's fine. I'll see you in there."

Jen darted down the narrow hallway to her office, closed the door behind her, and threw her notebook and pen on the desk. She scrolled through the contacts on her cell and clicked on Meg's number.

"Meg," Jen said breathlessly. "I'm so sorry to call out of the blue like this, but it's urgent."

"You okay? Is it the board meeting?"

"Um, I think I am . . . I mean, we're ready to go. The meeting starts soon, but I just got a text from Shauna." Jen closed her eyes and tried to slow her rapid breathing. "Sorry, I'm just a little flustered here. There's a rumor that our director of logistics, Jerry, just accepted an offer from Hydral."

"Shit!" Meg responded. "Does Michelle know?"

"Not yet. It's just a rumor. I don't want to cause additional stress right before the board meeting. Crap . . . *Hydral*, Meg! The tech giant that started in books and now delivers any product you need at any time. Last night, the Hydral site reminded me that I needed plastic bags! And of course, like an idiot, I ordered them because I know they'll arrive today, before I would've had a chance to get to the store." Jen plopped down in her desk chair. "What am I going to do?"

"Jen, listen to me. You are less than one hour away from an extremely critical meeting for you and for Dominal. Just take a deep breath and focus on the board meeting. This is still just a rumor, and you don't have time to validate it right now."

"You don't understand! This is our rock star, the guy that keeps everything together. We're screwed if we lose him!" Jen shook her head.

"It's okay. Listen, there's nothing you can do between now and the board meeting. Right now, just focus on being ready. This can wait until after. You don't even know if it's true yet. Take a deep breath," Meg encouraged her.

"Shauna wouldn't have texted me if she wasn't sure." Jen sighed. "I don't understand. Why do these things keep happening? It's like I can never catch a break."

"Jen, you can't think about any of this right now. Just focus on the board meeting," Meg said firmly.

"Yeah, I guess you're right. I only have forty minutes."

"Would it help if we ran through your talking points one more time? I have a break between meetings and was just eating lunch. I can certainly multitask."

"That would be great." Jen took a deep breath and once again went through her key talking points with Meg.

"You nailed it!" Meg exclaimed. "There's no doubt in my mind you're ready and are going to do great. Text me after the meeting."

"Thanks. I really, really appreciate this! Time to head to the boardroom. I'll keep you posted." Jen hung up and took another deep breath. She pulled the hem of her short, black blazer, collected her materials, and gathered her confidence as she walked down the hallway to the boardroom.

"You got this," she whispered to herself.

Two hours later, the doors to the boardroom swung open. After a few final handshakes, Mark, Michelle, and Renata spilled out into the hallway and made a sharp turn, walking briskly to Mark's office for an offline conversation. Mark's assistant guided the rest of the board members the other direction, toward the lobby.

Allan caught up to Jen as she was heading back toward her office.

"Hey, my friend, you did great in there!" Allan fist-bumped Jen a few feet away from her office door. "I'm proud of you."

"Thanks, Mr. Chang, right back at you! You nailed the finance stuff." Jen ushered Allan into her office and shut the door. She made her way to her desk and put her papers down. "But I have to admit, I was a bit surprised when Renata said that if we don't hit our six-month goals, Gold will take action to sell the company. It's unnerving."

Allan sighed and took a seat in Jen's guest chair. "Yeah, the bottom line is their investment thesis won't make sense if we don't at least hit those numbers. I get it."

Jen sat down in her office chair. "I get it too. But it's still hard to hear, and I can't even think about the implications for the team and our employees. Tell me the truth. Do you think we can do it?"

Allan cast his eyes down and dug his shoe into the fraying carpet. "Look, it's hard to tell. I think we've laid out a good starting plan, but we need to execute—and execute *well*—and continue to refine."

Jen slumped down in her chair, propped her elbows on the desk, and exhaled deeply.

"Look, don't be down about this. Celebrate the victories of the day!" Allan sat on the edge of the chair. "The meeting today went phenomenally well, and we've got some breathing room to execute. And once again, you did a fantastic job and should be really proud of yourself."

Jen relaxed a bit. "Thanks, that means a lot coming from you."

Allan stood up. "Let's get out of here. Neither of us have had a lot of time with family these past few weeks."

"Yeah, I've missed them." Jen smoothed her brown hair and slowly stood up from her chair.

"Well, once again, you did great today." Allan hugged her.

"Thanks, my friend!"

"Say hi to Davey." Allan waved. "And give the kids a hug from Uncle A!"

"Will do!" Jen beamed. "Send my love to Mindy and the kids."

Jen turned back to her desk and dialed Dave's cell number from her office speaker phone. She started to pack papers and her computer into her laptop bag.

"Hey, everything went fine," Jen said after her husband picked up. "I think we've got some breathing room from the board. I'm leaving now. Do you want me to pick up dinner?"

"The kids want to go to Chuck E. Cheese," Dave replied.

"You're kidding!" Jen rolled her eyes.

"Nope."

"Honey"—Jen zipped up her laptop bag—"I thought we agreed that we wouldn't take the kids there during the week."

"Well, they've been really good," Dave said persuasively. "I just think they deserve a treat."

"Great. They can have a scoop of ice cream tonight. Let's try to stay consistent with them . . . please?" Jen sighed audibly.

"Fine, I'll order food from home."

"Thanks. Oh, and can you please make sure you order something low carb for me? I'm on my way."

Jen hit the end button on her speakerphone. She picked up her purse and laptop bag, grabbed her keys, and exited her office. In the hallway, she stopped and pressed her face against the large interior windows that bordered the facility.

The facility was full of activity, and she saw Jerry out of the corner of her eye meeting with his supervisors and likely preparing for the upcoming shift change. She sighed, her heart heavy from the events of the day. She pulled her face back from the window and took out her cell to text Shauna: *Meeting went well. Thx for your help. Pls text me with any more news on Jerry.*

───────⟨◇⟩───────

Jen's whole mood changed for the better when she opened the front door of the Schmidt family bungalow and her kids, Cooper and Kat, ran toward her, nearly tackling her in the entryway. With them both clinging to her, she slowly passed the cozy living room and dining room and entered the kitchen, where her husband was taking out plates for dinner.

Jen gave him a tired kiss on the cheek and whispered, "Hi, honey. Thanks for ordering food."

Since Jen's parents' recent move to Florida, Dave had taken on a lot of extra duties. She missed her mom and dad and all the support they'd provided. Thankfully, Dave had arrived home at a decent hour today. He was still settling into his new job at Advantage Engineering, but luckily, he had flexibility right now.

After Jen had changed into her favorite Cubs sweatshirt and jeans, she and Dave set the table for dinner.

"Jen, can you do bath time and tuck in?" Dave grabbed the napkins.

"Can't you handle that?" Jen put the silverware down and checked her phone. No new texts.

"I *have* handled it for the last few weeks so you could focus on this board presentation," Dave snapped. "And tonight, I *need* to send a few emails before it's too late. Plus, the kids would like to spend a bit of time with their mom."

"Yeah, okay, you're right." Jen gave Dave a tired smile. "I'm sorry."

"Everything okay?" Dave asked.

"Yeah, yeah, just tired from today." Jen rubbed Dave's cheek. "It was intense."

The kids talked excitedly throughout dinner, filling Jen in on all the latest events at school. After dinner, Dave cleaned up while Jen helped the kids with their baths.

"Guess what, Kat? Tonight, it's your turn to pick the bedtime story." Jen mustered her last ounce of energy after bath time and used it to read Kat's choice, *Harry the Dirty Dog*—an old story that Jen's parents had read to her when she was young.

"Mommy," Cooper began, "how'd they not know it was Harry? Just 'cause he was dirty, they thought he was another dog?"

At five years old, Cooper was questioning bedtime stories more and more. Jen missed the good old days when he was simply mesmerized by the pictures.

Jen pulled the bedcovers over him. "Great question, Coop. Sometimes we just get caught up with looking at what's on the outside and forget to remember that it's what's on the *inside* that makes us who we are. Make sense?"

"I guess," Cooper replied.

When Jen tucked Kat into bed, she noticed her daughter's pajamas were growing tighter. She made a note to go shopping this weekend to get her little girl some new pajamas.

Jen tenderly kissed both children good night, turned off the light, and closed the bedroom door. She walked down the hallway, stopping to straighten out the forest green hallway rug that her in-laws had given them as a housewarming gift two years ago. She paused at the top of the stairs and checked her phone. Meg had texted her *Congrats on the meeting*, but there was nothing more from Shauna. Jen took a deep breath, making her way downstairs.

Out of the corner of her eye, she saw Dave opening a bottle of wine and noticed he had lit the wood-burning fireplace in the family room. The flames enhanced the unique perspectives of the Chicago landmarks Jen had painted and hung on the walls. Dave handed his wife a glass of wine when she entered the room. The couple spread out on a few oversized pillows on their slightly scuffed hardwood floor, which Jen refused to polish, insisting that it was part of the charm of the old house.

Dave raised his wine glass. "Here's to your successful meeting!"

"Thanks." Jen clinked her glass against his and took a sip. "Wow, you pulled out the cabernet that we got at the art show last month. I thought we were going to save it for a special occasion."

"Well, today is special. It's not every day that you nail a board presentation. You worked so hard on this. You deserve a bit of a celebration. Plus, you always pull out the expensive stuff when I have a work victory." Dave gently elbowed Jen's ribs. "Now, it's your turn! Tell me about your meeting."

"Yes, you will never convince me that we can celebrate something drinking PBR." Jen smirked and took a long sip of wine. "Seriously, Dave, for the first time I felt like we really came together as a cohesive team. I mean, Mark really did his part—he led the discussion with confidence, but not arrogance, and answered every question on target. My part went fine. I was ready. I'd gone through the key themes with Meg enough."

"Did they ask you any questions?"

"Yeah, for the first time ever, they really dug into my presentation." Jen stretched her neck. "They wanted a lot more details. And, of course, they wanted to give me their recommendations for external recruiters." Jen rolled her eyes.

Dave laughed and shook his head. "Some things never change. How did Allan do?"

"I thought he nailed the financials." Jen cupped her her wine glass.

"The board asked some tough questions, but he hung in there."

"Finance guys always nail it. This is what we live for." Dave swirled the wine in his glass. "What about the rest of the team?"

"Everyone did well." Jen pulled on her Cubs sweatshirt. "You're not going to believe this, but Michelle managed to sit still throughout the whole meeting."

"No way!" Dave nearly spat out his wine. "That must've taken all of her willpower."

"Yeah, we were all pretty surprised." Jen laughed. "But she did great in the meeting. You know, Michelle just has a way with people. When she says something, it's thoughtful, and people really respect it. Her initiatives were clear, and most of the board members were impressed. But you know Renata went so deep into the efficiency stuff. They actually had to take it offline after the meeting. Renata looked like she had the energy to go for another couple of hours."

"Dang, that's hard." Dave shifted so he was sitting cross-legged on the pillow. "Especially when you've been prepping like you guys have for the last few weeks."

Jen's cell buzzed, and she shot up to look at it. Not Shauna. She put the phone down and tried to settle down again. The wine was helping. "Yeah, I felt for her and Mark. They were still in Mark's office when I left. And Rich, well, you know . . . he cleans up well. He was articulate and sharp, and the board was impressed with the new sales channels he identified. I guess this is the side of Rich the customers get." She smiled and raised her empty glass to Dave, a quiet request for a refill.

"Yeah, he's a trip. But you think you bought some time?" Dave got up to refill their glasses.

"Yeah, I guess. They were clear that we have six months to turn this around. But they seemed to feel genuinely positive about the action plan." Jen's phone buzzed again, and she grabbed it immediately. Spam call.

"Okay, what's going on with the phone? Why are you so distracted? I thought we were celebrating."

"We are, it's just . . . Jerry might have an offer from Hydral."

"Oh, jeez. That would be a big blow."

"Yeah, believe me, I know." Jen sighed.

Jen felt Dave's gaze on her as she moved about the room. "You okay? Did you talk to Michelle or Mark?"

"It's just a lot all at once. I haven't told anyone yet. It's still a rumor. Plus, they rushed off with Renata right after the meeting. Why the hell do these things keep happening? I mean, seriously, I feel like I just can't catch a break."

Dave massaged Jen's shoulders. "You're really tense."

"I know. Ah, thanks . . . yeah, that feels great. I'm just frustrated . . . and nervous. I don't know what I am going to say to Michelle and Mark if Jerry takes the job. Hydral, of all places! Who would've thought a manufacturing firm like ours could lose talent to a tech giant?" Jen closed her eyes and moved her head back, grateful for Dave's touch.

Her phone buzzed again. *Shauna Miller.* Jen glanced up at her husband, a plea for moral support and perhaps another glass of wine, depending on the message.

"It's Shauna, isn't it?" he asked. "What did she say?"

Jen inhaled deeply and opened the text message: *It's true. We lost him to Hydral.*

She shoved the phone aside, no longer interested in anything else it had to offer. It was as though her chest had collapsed on itself, making it impossible to breathe. Yes, another glass of wine would be in order. "He took the job at Hydral," she said at last, shaking her head slowly. "I can't believe it. He took it!"

"Sorry, honey. Come here." Dave put his arm around her waist and pulled her a bit closer.

"Thanks," Jen whispered in his ear. "It's still early in California. I think I should text Meg."

"What about Michelle? Should you give her a heads-up, as a friend?"

"I don't know." Jen pulled away from Dave and shook her head. "I think she needs to hear this from Jerry—it's his news to share."

"Okay, well, see what Meg says." Dave gave Jen a reassuring look. "I'm going to head upstairs and read a bit. You coming up soon?"

"Yeah, just give me a few minutes. I'll put out the fire before I head up." Jen grabbed her phone and started texting Meg: *Jerry going to Hydral—confirmed.*

She walked back into the kitchen and poured the last bit of wine into her glass.

A minute later, there was a response from Meg: *Breathe. One step at a time.* Before Jen could respond, she got another text from Meg: *Wine? Edibles? Just kidding. Or maybe not?*

Despite the tension she felt all over her body, Jen laughed out loud and texted back, *Cab is doing the trick.* She appreciated Meg's ability to read her mood.

Meg sent a smile emoji and added, *Seriously, nothing you can do tonight. Get some rest. We'll tackle it in the morning.*

CHAPTER 6

"HAVE A GOOD day, Dave. Thanks again for taking the kids to school. Make sure they wear their mittens, please!" Jen grabbed a yogurt from the from the refrigerator and stuffed it into her laptop bag just after a quarter past six.

"Good luck," a barely awake Dave mumbled as he poured his first cup of coffee.

She gave Dave a kiss on the check. She waved at him and headed to the entryway, her brown stilettos stumbling over Kat's toys in the living room. She grabbed her black coat, swung it over her tan business suit, and tied a light pink scarf around her neck.

Jen was eager to arrive at the office early and get a jump on things. She and Meg were set to talk in a few hours, and Jen wanted time to further analyze Hydral's plans to open a warehouse and distribution center in the local area.

Fifteen minutes later, as she took the last sip of coffee from her travel mug, Jen was walking toward her office and caught a glimpse of Michelle dressed in dark jeans, a red sweater, and light brown, steel-toed warehouse boots. Michelle's typically pristine blonde hair was pulled back in a messy ponytail, which must have meant she had been on site for the four o'clock shift.

She paced back and forth in front of Jen's desk, her arms crossed so tightly, it was a miracle she could still breathe. Jen took a deep breath and braced herself for the conversation.

"Hey, Michelle." Jen avoided eye contact while she made her way to her desk and placed her laptop bag down with a slight bang.

"You're not going to believe this." Michelle stopped in her tracks and faced Jen. "Jerry just resigned! He got an offer from Hydral to run logistics for their local warehouse! What the hell?!"

"Yeah, I caught wind of a rumor yesterday but didn't want to say anything until we knew for sure." Jen shook her head. "I'm sorry, Michelle."

"C'mon Jen, we're friends! Why didn't you let me know?"

"It was just a rumor until late last night." Jen sighed. "I knew you'd had a long day with the board, and then straight into a meeting with Renata. I didn't want to worry you until I knew for sure. Also, it's a bit awkward . . . I mean, it's his news to share."

"Well, I never expected a company like Hydral to poach our talent!" Michelle threw up her arms and continued pacing. "For shit's sake, how do we compete with them? Hydral! Ugh. They can have any talent in the world, and they know it. Jerry is the best director of logistics around—he's the magic that makes our facility work! How the hell are we going to survive without him?!"

"Yeah, this is a tough one." Jen sat in her office chair. "Maybe you should—"

"A *tough one?* That's all you have to say?! I need more than your sympathy right now. You're the head of HR. This is your deal! You need to have a plan here! We can't keep losing talent like this!" Michelle stormed out of Jen's office.

Jen slumped in her chair and blinked back tears. For the first time, she wondered if this was all worth it. How the hell was she going to compete with a company like Hydral? She closed her eyes and tried to compose herself. "One step at a time," she said out loud. She opened her eyes and a new browser tab, and typed H-y-d-r-a-l. It was time to figure out how this monster of a company was going to impact Dominal's future.

Still deep in research several hours later, Jen was staring intently at her monitor. She didn't even notice Shauna plop down in one of the guest chairs across from her desk.

After about 20 seconds, Shauna cleared her throat, and Jen finally looked up. "Oh, sorry, Shauna. I'm deep in Hydral world. What's up?"

"Well, it's nine thirty. Are we still on for our regular one-on-one?"

"Of course, yes. I totally lost track of time."

"Are you okay? Is this about Jerry?"

"Of course it is." Jen rubbed her forehead. "Jerry finally told Michelle this morning and she was pretty upset . . . at me."

"Well, like I texted you last night, it's an offer he couldn't refuse. Hydral?! Can you *imagine*? He doesn't have to move, doubles the size of his team, gets a nice pay raise and stock in a leading company. Plus, he now has Hydral on his resume!"

"Well, Hydral isn't all it's cracked up to be. It's tough over there. Remember that article about their harsh culture a few years ago?"

"Maybe, but their Glassdoor rating is higher than ours." Shauna leaned forward in her chair and lowered her voice. "But seriously, there's no way we can compete with Hydral. People need to adjust their expectations."

"That's not going to fly with Michelle." Jen spoke in an equally low tone. "Shauna, did you ever think we'd be losing talent to big tech companies?"

"To be honest, no. It never really crossed my mind." Shauna repositioned herself in the chair. "But I guess they have to distribute products just like we do."

"Well, I can't just tell Michelle to deal with it. Not with the board breathing down our necks. Jerry was key talent and amazing at what he did. This is a big loss. I texted Meg last night, and we're going to connect over Zoom later this morning. I'm hopeful she'll have some words of wisdom."

⟨————⟩

"Meg, it's bad, really bad." Jen scraped the bottom of her yogurt container to get the last bite. "Sorry, I left the house at the crack of dawn, and this is the first chance I've had to eat."

"Hang on, give me a sec. I need to change positions here." Meg pulled her jeans up slightly and straightened her red-and-white flannel shirt when she stood up. "Sorry, my back's been hurting, so I don't want to sit too long. Okay, I'm good. So, tell me more about Hydral's expansion."

"Well, the news isn't good. I mean, it's good for our city—it means a ton of new jobs—but this is going to be hell for Dominal. We're already strained, and now we'll have to fight to keep our people. And Shauna is right too—despite all the press about its culture, Hydral still has a higher Glassdoor rating than us." Jen took the last bite of her yogurt and tossed the container in the trash.

"How's Michelle taking it?" Meg stretched her Slinky back and forth like an accordion. "Hope you don't mind, you know the Slinky helps me think."

Jen quickly tipped her head to the side. "She's really upset."

"Well, that's to be expected. Try not to take it personally."

"Yeah, but it's only going to get worse. Hydral plans to open another warehouse in the city next year. Everyone is at risk. A tech giant coming after our talent . . . this has to be a first, even for you!"

Meg shook her head. "Unfortunately not."

Jen straightened her back so it was flush against her chair. "What?"

"This has been happening for some time. Do you know who Shonda Rhimes is?"

"Um, yeah—the producer, right? *Grey's Anatomy, Scandal.*"

"Yes. She worked at ABC for over twenty years and decided to quit a few years ago. Do you know where she went?"

Jen shook her head.

"Netflix." Meg put her Slinky down. "There are a lot of stories like that. Back in 2015, Uber opened a lab around the corner from Carnegie Melon University and poached their entire robotics lab. Carnegie Melon was reeling."

"Wow, I had no idea!" Jen leaned into the screen. "They just come out of nowhere like that?"

"Yes. Those are just a few big examples." Meg took a sip of water. "Many of my clients outside of tech face similar challenges. When you think about it, tech companies have pervaded our lives, right? Google lets its employees spend up to twenty percent of their time working on innovation, so we don't really know where it's going to go next."

"I guess . . . ugh!" Jen turned away from the monitor to cast her glance at the abstract art in her office.

"Well, the reality is every company is competing for talent against the tech giants now, whether they realize it or not. And let's face it, these guys know how to attract and retain talent."

Jen returned her gaze to the screen and rubbed her temples. "Okay, so why haven't you raised this issue before?"

"Well, we've been focused on the action plan, which was the first step to buy you some time with the board—but if you're going to hit those six-month targets, we're going to have to do more."

Jen sighed. "Okay."

"So, before today, who were your biggest competitors for talent?"

"Um, let's see . . . there's Meis and Turnstile. We go after their talent. They go after ours. It's a toss-up who wins."

"And what makes you different, from a company stand-point?" Meg looked ready to jot down notes.

Jen stretched her neck. "You know, we pay pretty much the same, and our benefits are pretty close. I think sometimes we pay a little more to get their talent and vice versa, but I'm not sure about a specific differentiator, per se."

"Hmm . . ." Meg tipped her head. "And how do your Glassdoor ratings compare?"

"No idea about their ratings, but we're about a 3.2, which I know isn't great."

"Well, it's all relative, right? If they're at a 1.0, then a 3.2, while not great, is still doing better than your competition."

"I doubt they are at a 1.0!" Jen smiled. "But yes, you're right. Although, I'm not sure why this matters?"

"All things being equal, why would someone come work for Dominal?" Meg sat back in her chair and adjusted her laptop to not lose eye contact with Jen.

"Well, despite our cutbacks, we have all of the HR best prac-tices implemented. I think that works in our favor." Jen tapped her desk with her pen twice to reinforce the point.

"But let's say that all your competitors have best practices implemented too. What makes Dominal unique?"

"I'm not sure I follow." Jen shook her head. "From an HR perspective, what's more important than best practices?"

"Well, best practices put you on a level playing field with your competitors, but they do nothing to differentiate you. Why would an employee choose your company over competitors?"

"I understand what you're saying in theory, but not sure that's what HR is really about. My focus has always been on those best practices. They're important," Jen argued.

"So, let's look at this a different way. Do you think Rich can focus on best practices *only* and expect to grow sales?"

"Of course not." Jen put her elbows on the desk. "But getting customers is so different than hiring people."

"It's interesting you'd say that." Meg inclined her head. "How? How is it different?"

Jen processed Meg's question for a few moments. "You know, I don't really know. It feels like it's different, but I can't tell you why."

"This is a somewhat new concept for HR." Meg smiled. "You can't have a cost center mindset where you solely focus on compliance. There is *always* competition for good talent. And these days, talent is a key part of a company's competitive advantage. I tell clients that attracting talent is no different than attracting customers."

Jen looked puzzled. "I don't follow."

"You need to be as thoughtful about acquiring employees as you are about customers." Meg pushed back in her chair and crossed her legs. "And here's the thing—most companies are deliberate about how they acquire customers. That's what keeps them alive. While you have some short-term struggles right now, in general, Dominal already knows how to attract customers. You now have to take those strategies and apply them to talent."

"I've never thought of it that way." Jen tapped her pen on the desk. "I mean, I've read about talent brands and employment value propositions, but what you're saying is different—another level."

"Think about it. A customer is just making a simple decision to buy your products, while an employee is making a decision to spend a good chunk of his or her waking hours with you, possibly for years. There's a lot more at stake."

"I guess that's true." Jen wrote some notes.

"Look," Meg explained, "the brand and value proposition are all good things, but they won't stick unless you have something behind it. You really need a unique HR strategy grounded in Dominal's business goals—one that differentiates your company and helps you compete for talent."

"Okay, so let's say we do this . . ." Jen's stomach growled, which reminded her that yogurt never really satisfies her hunger. "How is it even possible that we can build something compelling when we don't have the resources or funding that Hydral does?"

"Great question." Meg smiled broadly. "When it comes down to it, it's not about the perks or the money. If you're focused on the right things, on treating people right, on building something meaningful and compelling, people will want to be part of it. People crave meaning, even more than money. With the right mission, vision, and values, you can compete against the Hydrals of this world, I promise you."

"You make it sound so simple!" Jen exclaimed.

"Well, no, it's not simple." Meg chuckled. "But most companies don't take the time to do it . . . so if *you* take the time to do it, you'll have a strong competitive advantage."

"I don't know." Jen held her head in her hands, her elbows on the desk. "I get we must compete for talent with giants like Hydral, but I just don't know what the leadership team will think of this." She shook her head. "But I guess we don't really have a choice."

"There's rarely a small solution to a big problem." Meg picked up her Slinky again and stretched it across her desk.

"Okay, Meg, you win. So, what do I do next?"

"Excellent!" Meg toward her computer screen. "First, you've got to get the lay of the land. I want you to comb through your business strategy and make sure you fully understand where Dominal is trying to go and what the people implications are. Then, I want you to read every review on Glassdoor about Dominal."

"*Every* review?" Jen questioned.

"Yes, *every* review. You need to go deep and pull out key themes. What are the positive and negative things people are saying about Dominal? This will help you figure out what you need to fix as well as what you need to amplify in your strategy.

What are they saying about your interview process, your competitors' interview processes, and so on?"

"Okay." Jen made a few more notes.

"Then read the last year's reviews for your top three competitors. This will give you a picture of what their key positive and negative themes are and help you start to home in on what makes Dominal unique."

Jen sighed, but continued to jot down notes.

"Next, I want you to spend time with each of the folks on the leadership team. Really dig into what's keeping them up at night and how we can address it from a people perspective."

"They are really busy, Meg. They're not going to have time for this."

Jen looked down at her lap so she didn't have to see Meg's stern look.

"Then you have to push them to make time, Jen. This is important. I think you know that." Meg leaned even closer to her monitor. "You can't do this in a vacuum. You need input from everyone on the leadership team to build something meaningful for Dominal. You need all the stakeholders on board. I have a list of sample questions I'll send you to keep these discussions business focused."

"Okay." Jen looked back to the monitor. "The questions would be a big help."

"From there, I want you to organize everything you learn into four quadrants: Dominal's strengths, weaknesses, opportunities, and external threats."

"A SWOT analysis." Jen jotted down more notes. "I've seen those before but never thought about applying it to HR. Okay, I will give it a shot."

An hour later, after Jen refueled on a grilled chicken salad and a bowl of turkey chili, she situated herself back at her desk and began to read Dominal's Glassdoor reviews. She was completely immersed when she was interrupted by a rap on her office door.

"Hey, sorry to bother you. You look like you're deep in thought again." Shauna was standing in her doorway.

Jen looked up from her screen. "Uh, yeah . . . I was just reviewing something. What's up?"

"Well, I just need you to approve the Lighthouse invoice we discussed earlier today."

"Give me a quick sec. I will take care of it now." Jen logged into the billing system. "Shauna, just curious, how many of our Glassdoor reviews have you read?"

"Um, quite a few. I check in on them from time to time to see what people are saying." Shauna sat down in Jen's guest chair. "Why do you ask?"

"Meg asked me to read every single one of them in depth. I just started digging into it." Jen approved the invoice online and turned her gaze to Shauna. "I have to admit, while I knew our rating wasn't great, I hadn't really taken the time to read what people were saying."

"What do you mean?" Shauna asked.

"All of these reviews people have posted—they say some harsh things about us."

"Um, Jen, with all due respect, our recruiting team raised this issue with you," Shauna said quietly.

Jen jerked her head back. "Well, I know the team mentioned it in passing . . ."

"It was more than in passing . . . the recruiting team raised it again just a few weeks ago." Shauna tilted her head. "It seemed like you didn't want to engage with the topic."

"What? I'm sorry if I gave you that impression." Jen shook her head in embarrassment. She had always prided herself on being a good listener, and she couldn't believe she didn't grasp the severity of the situation her team had raised. "I guess . . . I just didn't realize. This is just . . . well, it's tough to read."

"Yeah, imagine if you're recruiting, and candidates are asking you about it." Shauna stood up. "Um, I gotta run to meet with my team. Thanks for approving the invoice."

"Yeah, no worries," Jen mumbled. "Thanks again."

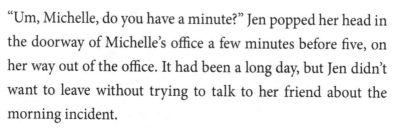

"Um, Michelle, do you have a minute?" Jen popped her head in the doorway of Michelle's office a few minutes before five, on her way out of the office. It had been a long day, but Jen didn't want to leave without trying to talk to her friend about the morning incident.

Michelle was standing at her whiteboard, furiously scribbling. "Oh, hi. Yep, I was actually about to head over to your office. Have a seat." She gestured to the small, round conference table in her office.

Jen put her laptop bag and purse down on the floor, taking in all the framed pictures of the warehouse operations in action. There was something so unique about the angles of the shots. Jen made a note to try to draw some of these the next time she had time to paint.

Michelle took a seat across from her and placed her hands on the table. "Hey, I'm sorry about earlier. I shouldn't have lost my cool. I just was totally shocked about Jerry."

"It's okay," Jen replied, avoiding eye contact.

"No, it's not." Michelle ducked her head to try to look Jen in the eye. "It's never okay for any of us to talk like that to each other. We're a team here, we have to stick together, especially right now. I can disagree or even provide feedback, but not in an angry way. That's not who I am."

Jen smiled. She truly admired Michelle's humility. In a short time, Michelle had earned the respect of everyone at all levels of Dominal, and Jen suspected it was from her ability to listen and learn from everyone and every situation.

"You're right—and it's also not the culture we want to build. Thank you for your apology, I appreciate it."

Michelle smiled. "If it weren't so crazy right now, I'd say let's go grab a drink—but I know we were both in here early, and I don't think our families would be very understanding, especially given how little time we've spent with them lately."

"Yeah. Dave is going out with his buddies later this week. And to be honest, I am actually a little happy he'll be out of the house so I can get a couple more hours of work in after putting the kids to bed." Jen sighed. "What's wrong with me?"

"Ugh, I know what you mean." Michelle shook her head. "This shit's out of control. You hanging in there?"

Jen gave a half smile. "Yeah, I am. Meg's been a big help. I can't believe I was pushing off working with her. What about you?"

"You know, I'm not sure." Michelle folded her hands on the table. "Jerry is such a huge loss, but I've stopped the poor me routine, and I'm trying to figure out how to move forward."

"Look, I want to help with that. You're right—this is just as much my problem. If we put our heads together, we can figure something out. Plus, it'll give me a chance to get a better understanding of some of our key talent and operations."

"That would be great." Michelle gave her a weary smile. "I would welcome the help."

"Yeah, and, uh . . . actually, I stopped by to also let you know I'm working on a comprehensive plan to deal with Hydral. I know we can't sit back and lose more talent. I will share more during tomorrow's leadership meeting."

"I look forward to it." Michelle unfolded her hands and hoisted herself up to gather her things. "Well, I've actually decided to take the night off. There's nothing more I can do. I'm exhausted, and I think I'm going to watch the Cubs game tonight. A little time with Joe and the kids will help me think more clearly tomorrow. Assuming we don't all end up fighting after five minutes!"

Jen laughed. "Yeah, Dave and I are going to watch the game too. I'm just hoping he doesn't make me drink PBR with him. There are limits! I'll walk out with you."

———⌁———

At 10:50 the next morning, Jen made her way to the boardroom. She knew that the topic of Jerry would come up, and she wanted to be ready to address and share her new approach with the leadership team. She straightened her blue pantsuit and situated herself at the conference room table. While she waited for the rest of the team to arrive, she stared out at the light dusting of snow covering the adjacent building.

Rich sauntered in eight minutes later, loudly chewing gum. "Well, look who's the first one here today."

"Hi, Rich. Trying to change my ways." Jen smiled with the same sarcastic look she always had ready for Rich and his snide comments.

"Okay, everyone," Mark started when the rest of the team arrived a few minutes later. "Any big issues we want to discuss?"

Michelle got straight to the point. "So, I know you've all heard about Jerry and Hydral. . ."

"Yeah, I lost sleep last night over it." Mark sighed and adjusted his glasses. "I want to talk to him today and dig into this a bit more. We need to see if he's salvageable; we're already facing an uphill battle to meet the board's six-month targets, so we need to try to save him."

"You should talk to him." Michelle shifted in her chair. "But don't get your hopes up, he's not going to budge. It's Hydral, the opportunity of a lifetime for him. We just can't compete against these tech giants; the prestige alone is huge and will open so many doors for him, not to mention the stock will likely change his life."

"Surely there's something we can do." Mark shifted his glance to Jen. "What do you think?"

"I agree with Michelle—it's worth it for you to talk to him, but this is Hydral. I doubt you can change his mind. Still, he's a valued employee and has done so much for us—we all owe it to talk to him and treat him with dignity and respect," Jen said confidently. "And I think we also need to focus on a bigger issue here. I spent some time analyzing the impact of Hydral's plans yesterday. I know you're aware they're creating a bunch of new jobs in the area—which is great for our community, but the reality is that this is going raise several challenges for us. I'd like to discuss this."

"Okay, go ahead, Jen." Mark pulled up the sleeves of his brown sweater.

"Well, you guys know I am working with Meg Beecham, the HR consultant, right? Well, yesterday, she helped me understand that the talent market has fundamentally shifted, and HR must use the same rigor to attract talent that we apply to attracting customers." Jen glanced around the room at the curious expressions on everyone's faces. "I am working on an overall HR approach to do this, based on our business strategy. This will help differentiate us as a company. It will be a complete shift away from the traditional compliance focus we've had to date. Going forward, I want us to focus on things that really make a difference in helping us with our business goals."

Mark's adjusted his glasses. The rest of the team was silent as they looked around uncomfortably at each other.

"What? Why is everyone so quiet? You look like you just saw a ghost."

"Jen, sorry, I'm just going to be blunt here," Rich started. "Attracting customers is an entirely different ball game. Your team doesn't have any experience here. How are you going to apply customer acquisition strategies to talent?"

Jen squirmed in her chair but continued to listen. She knew this would be a hard sell and reminded herself to keep her professional poker face.

"You know, we all want to see you and your team succeed," Allan added softly. "This is a big change. I could be wrong, but I'm not even sure I've seen the HR team out in the facility, even though it's the bread and butter of our operations."

"Look, I realize what we're doing now is not enough." Jen glanced around the room. "We have to stop being so reactive to everything. With Hydral coming in, we're now going to fight much harder to keep our talent and compete for new talent. I started digging into our Glassdoor reviews and those of our competitors. It's a wealth of information that I should've been focused on all along."

Michelle stood up from her chair. "I think we need to give this a shot. It took a lot of courage for Jen to come in and admit that we need a change of direction. We should support this, and

I personally will make time. We can't afford to lose more great talent—and with our board targets and Hydral coming in, well, we have to do more in this space."

Mark cleared his throat. "Agreed. We brought Meg in to challenge our thinking in this area, and she's doing just that through her work with us. We need bold moves to be able to avoid a sale in six months." He stroked his chin. "Jen, you're going to need to get much deeper with each of the leaders. Spend some time with Michelle in the facility, go on a sales call with Rich, dig into Allan's financial projections. This is the only way you can really understand our business challenges."

"Yeah, I know I can't build this alone, and it's going to take time. I really need to understand the challenges from all of your perspectives. I'm generating a list of questions for each of you, so I'll come prepared. I promise to make the most of your time."

"Sorry, Jen, I want to support you, but I don't have a lot of time right now." Rich sighed. "There's too much pressure in sales. And Mark, I just don't think I can position Jen to come to a sales call. How would I explain it?"

"Rich, we have to give this a shot," Mark interjected gruffly. "That's enough on this. I expect everyone to make time for Jen in the coming weeks, no exceptions."

———————— ∾◇∾ ————————

A little before eight thirty that evening, Jen picked out her favorite pinot noir from the built-in wine rack in her kitchen. She poured herself a glass and walked through the small entryway to the dining room. Setting her glass down on the well-loved, dark oak dining room table around which her family had gathered so often during her childhood, she opened her laptop and went back to Glassdoor.

She stretched her neck as she settled in to read a few more reviews, sighing heavily as she read and sipped the remaining half glass of wine. She grabbed her cell phone and made her way into the kitchen.

Sorry to text so late, Meg. Self-medicating with wine while I read Glassdoor reviews. Jen topped off her glass and stood at the kitchen window, staring out into the darkness.

Her phone buzzed with a text back from Meg. *They can be rough. You okay?*

Jen looked up at the ceiling and blinked back tears of exhaustion. She took a deep breath. *Not really,* she admitted in her reply text.

The phone buzzed right away. *Can you get on Zoom right now?*

Yes. Pls send link, Jen texted back.

Jen slugged back to the dining room and logged into Zoom. "Thanks, Meg," Jen said gently.

"Hey, no worries! It's only six thirty here, and I was looking for an excuse to have a beer. Hope it's okay if I join you virtually." Meg raised her glass of lager.

Jen managed a smile. "Of course, but you may need to catch up—I am starting my second glass!"

"Hmm . . . don't challenge me. I can keep up with the best of them." Meg laughed. "I figured you would be wearing a Cubs sweatshirt."

"Yeah, it's my go-to outfit at home. Gosh, there's nothing better than jeans, a Cubs sweatshirt, and UGGs." Jen lifted her leg to show Meg her calf-high boots.

"Nice! I love UGGs, too, but it's not cold enough here in LA." Meg sipped her beer.

Jen read the phrase on Meg's shirt. " 'Surely not everyone was kung fu fighting'?" She smiled. "Clever."

"My brother got me the shirt last year for my birthday. I absolutely love it, but I know it's not really politically correct these days. I don't wear it for client meetings, but this is more of a virtual happy hour, right?" Meg winked.

"Definitely." Jen lifted her wine glass with a smile.

"So, this is your dining room, huh?" Meg moved her head toward the monitor to get a closer view of the oak chair rail and dark red walls that framed the room. "Those paintings behind you are phenomenal. Are they yours?"

"Yep."

Jen glanced behind her at the various oil paintings that hung in a single row on each wall of the room. The dining room was her absolute favorite room in the house. She and Dave wanted one nicer space in their home to entertain family and friends and host holidays. They'd spent a lot of time planning the décor, striving for both simplicity and elegance. After much debate, she and Dave settled on the paintings they loved the most and had them professionally framed. Jen felt a sense of pride every time she looked around the room.

"And this"—Jen lightly slapped her hands down on the dining table—"belonged to my parents. They gave us theirs when we bought the house because I just loved it so much. And it's really nice now, since they're no longer close by. Listen, the next time you're in Chicago, you have to come over for dinner."

"I'd love that." Meg smiled. "I'm also in my dining room, but it's a bit smaller and no homemade art. I am a terrible artist! We did one of those paint and alcohol things last year, and mine turned out so bad. And that was after my artist friend tried to fix it!"

Jen laughed. "Okay, we'll keep painting off the list of activities when you're in town."

"So, tell me, what's driving you to self-medicate?"

"Well, Dave is out with his buddies, and the kids are asleep, so I thought I would dig back into the Glassdoor reviews." Jen began to massage her forehead. "Honestly, Meg, I had no idea. I can't believe what people are saying about us. I knew our rating was low, but I guess I never took the time to really understand why."

"Yeah, like I said, they can be rough." Meg slowly bobbed her head. "When I try to talk to potential clients about them, a lot of them discount the reviews because they feel they are from bitter employees—but it's the only thing out there that employees are saying. We wouldn't treat bad customer reviews like that, would we?"

"You're right." Jen tapped the stem of her wine glass. "I'm guilty of doing the same thing. But reading them through the lens of trying to find patterns and themes makes me see how valuable this stuff is. There are plenty of examples of how our managers aren't living up to Dominal's values and how employees aren't feeling the culture we describe."

"I see this at a lot of companies. The good news is you can fix this."

"You know, sometimes I can even figure out who said it, which just makes it worse." Jen cast her glance down. "And Shauna told me the recruiting team has been raising the Glassdoor issue for a while. She said it seemed like I didn't want to engage." She shook her head.

"Listen to me, you can't beat yourself up for what you didn't do in the past." Meg leaned toward the monitor. "You're paying attention to it now, and you're going to fix it and use it as a tool going forward."

"But we've left all of these reviews out there with no acknowledgement." Jen sighed. "I can't believe we never responded. It makes us look . . . I don't know . . . foolish."

"It's never too late to respond to reviews. But first, figure out what you're going to do to address the bigger problem. Then, make sure you address every review authentically, with a balance of business and compassion, just like you would for a customer review. A canned response will make the situation worse."

"That makes sense."

"Look, I know this is hard, but I am really proud of the way you're stepping up to this challenge and committing to change." Meg smiled. "Everyone has turning points or events in their lives that make them look at things differently. You know, I've stumbled so many times. I've fallen flat on my face over and over . . . hell, I still do, all the time. Running your own business comes with a whole new set of challenges! And while it's hard when you're going through it, you just gotta know that you're going to learn something valuable from it."

Jen rolled back her shoulders. "Yeah, I hope you're right."

"I gotta couple years on you and on this—I *know* I'm right." Meg took a sip of her beer. "Listen, my friend, turn it off for tonight. Go relax a bit. Paint, watch some TV, maybe have another glass of wine. You need to lighten up a bit. Hell, if it's your thing, *light up.*"

Jen laughed. "Why do you always offer that up? Is it *your* thing?"

"No, but you'd think it would be, right?" Meg laughed. "Living in California, going to college at Berkeley. But no, it's not my thing. I just love to tease people about it. I am strictly a beer girl."

"A beer-drinking poet who transforms HR and dabbled in finance. You're definitely an original." Jen smiled. "Okay, I'll do some painting before bed. Thanks for everything. Talk to you tomorrow. 'Night."

CHAPTER 7

"WHAT DO YOU think?" Jen popped open her takeout container and dug her fork into her fettucine alfredo.

Shauna turned her head. "I thought you were low carb?"

Jen sighed. "*I am.* I decided to forgo the diet until we have the leadership team signed off on the new strategy. Think of it as self-care."

"Whatever works." Shauna rolled her eyes and took a bite of her salad. "I think we've captured most of the key themes from your interviews and Glassdoor, but are these really the things we should be focused on? We don't talk about benefits at all."

"I think so." Jen stood up and took her gray suit jacket from the back of her chair and put it back on. "When I asked them why they are excited to come to work, nearly all our facility team members talked about how they're proud that they keep people safe and healthy and how we're always looking for ways to make a better product. We're pretty direct on the management challenges and inefficiencies in the warehouse too."

"Don't get me wrong, I really like it. It's a great business SWOT." Shauna tapped her fork on the table. "But I think we'll have some convincing to do that it's the right place for us to start building an HR strategy."

Jen took another bite of her pasta. She and Shauna had spent the last couple of days holed up in the HR conference room, working long hours to interpret the data from the interviews and Glassdoor. Mark had released her from every meeting not related to the strategy. Her phone buzzed, and she glanced down to read the text.

"Is everything okay?" Shauna dabbed her napkin on the dressing she had spilled on her blue sweater.

"Yeah, it's Dave. He's just telling me he got the kids to bed. He knows I worry about not being there for bedtime." Jen texted back a heart emoji.

"That's sweet." Shauna gave Jen a worn-out smile. "It's been a long few days. I'm looking forward to spending some quality time with Ravi when this is over—he's been really patient."

"Yeah, we're both lucky there. I owe Dave when this is over." Jen shook her head. "Look, Mark wants us to fix the business problems. We told everyone we're going to be bold, and this is our first step."

"Okay." Shauna put her hands behind her head. "Let's go with it."

"Awesome!" Jen put her hand up to high-five Shauna.

Shauna shook her head. "You need to lay off the carbs. You're way too perky for our twelfth hour of being in this conference room."

Jen laughed. "I can't help it, I'm excited!"

"More like delirious," Shauna countered with a smile.

━━━━━◇━━━━━

"Twenty-five, six, two, four . . . sixteen. Do you get it?" Meg nodded excitedly at the start of her Zoom call. Her gold sweater sparkled in the Los Angeles morning sun.

Jen and Shauna exchanged confused glances. They sat in the newly redesigned conference room right off the lobby of the building. The room was so different from the old HR conference room, where they had spent the last few days hammering out a new strategy. It was one of the few times that Jen and Rich had joined forces and successfully lobbied Mark to redecorate the room to provide customers and job candidates a strong first impression. In addition to the new bright blue carpet, light maple table, and silver-framed chairs, the room had been outfitted with all the latest technology, which was necessary for today's meeting with Meg.

"No! What?!" Jen shook her head. "I have no idea what that license plate means."

"So, years ago, there was a song by the band Chicago called '25 or 6 to 4.' I thought the twenty-five, six, two, four part could refer to Chicago and the sixteen to the year. Really, everything else is taken in California. You Cubs fans are spread out."

"It's more like pent-up demand. It just took us forever to break that curse, and by the time we did, Cubs fans had infiltrated the entire United States!" Shauna rested her chin in her hands. "So, what did your friend say when you suggested it?"

"Similar reaction to you two, plus an eye roll. But give it time . . . I promise it will be a cool license plate!" Meg's blue eyes sparkled. "Okay, so let's get back to the topic at hand. How were the rest of the interviews?"

"Good. I mean . . . wow, I learned a lot." Jen shuffled through her notes. "Especially in the facility. It was great to hear why people want to come to work every day. And the sales calls were interesting too. It was really cool to hear firsthand what customers think about when they buy from us."

"Gives you a whole other perspective, right?" Meg said. "Almost like how you paint. You take something like the Hancock Center and take a different view, change the lighting, and it's a whole new image."

"Yes, you're right! I guess I do that all the time. Hadn't thought about how that might apply to work." Jen glanced outside the conference room window at the gray, mid-autumn sky for a moment. "Shauna, can you please share the SWOT with Meg?"

Shauna shared her screen with Meg and let her read through the analysis.

"This is good . . . really good." Meg inclined her head. "You have a lot to work with. What did the leadership team think?"

"They all thought it was an accurate picture of where we are from a business and organization standpoint." Shauna smiled and looked at Jen, as though for affirmation. "Jen let me attend the meeting with her."

"Awesome. Now, we have something solid to work with. Knowing the lay of the land is critical to strategy. If you don't have a good grasp on that, you can't build effective programs."

Jen stood up and shed her black suit jacket and laid it on the chair next to her. "So, what's next, Meg?"

"It's time to start designing your strategy." Meg picked up her Slinky and twirled it on two fingers. "You now need to translate your business goals into a vision. You need a mission and some specific HR programs and services to support your mission. The SWOT will help you think this all through."

"What do you mean by vision?" Shauna was typing on her laptop as Meg spoke. "We already have a vision statement for Dominal—should our HR vision be different?"

"That's a good question." Meg put her Slinky down. "The company vision is what the company aspires to be. The HR vision is what HR aspires to be *within* the organization."

"Okay, I hear what you're saying, but how do we apply this to HR?" Jen looked puzzled. "Do you have an example of an HR vision?"

"Sure. It should be a bit aspirational. At a professional services firm, we came up with a vision 'to be the supply chain of the business.' Talent was our product—we were selling services. As HR, we find and cultivate talent, right?"

"Oohhh, I like that." Shauna looked up from her laptop to the large projection screen. "So simple and easy to remember."

"Exactly!" Meg smiled broadly. "By positioning ourselves this way, we changed the perception of our team as a back-office function to something that was relevant to the business. The key is to think about the greater purpose HR serves to customers and employees."

"Got it." Jen jotted down notes. "I'm really glad we did those customer meetings now. I can bring in their perspectives."

"Yeah, there were some tidbits in there that can help us." Shauna nodded. "Meg, what was the mission in the example you just gave?"

"Right—so the mission is how you will achieve the vision." Meg took a sip of water. "So, our mission was to have 'the right people in the right place at the right time.' This is exactly what a supply chain does—it ensures the product is available when there is demand. We wanted to be viewed the same way."

"Hmm . . . I really like that too." Jen rested her pen on the corner of her mouth. "The interesting part is there is no mention of things that are more traditional HR."

"As simple as it sounds now, it was extremely difficult to get people to agree to that." Meg chuckled. "Bold ideas always get pushback. It usually takes time for people to warm up to new ideas."

"How did you handle the pushback?" Jen asked.

"Not well. I was angry and took it personally that they didn't like my idea. I fought them because I felt I was right—which, as you can imagine, caused me to fall flat on my face," Meg admitted. "But as time went on, I learned that you have to take that pushback and turn it into feedback. It helps you refine and test your ideas. Think about the very first person to propose matching drivers with people who wanted a ride? Do you think everyone said 'great idea' right away? Probably not. But today, I'll be taking an Uber to my next meeting. It takes gumption to bring about change. You've got to push through the skepticism."

"Yeah!" Shauna clapped her hands together. "And now none of us think twice about ride-sharing."

"Or getting into a stranger's car," Jen chimed in.

"Right?!" Meg sat back in her chair. "So interesting how quickly things change."

"So, vision, mission . . . and then you said goals." Jen massaged her right shoulder, which had been sore after her weekend workout. "I assume these have to be in the language of the business?"

"Yep." Meg gave a thumbs-up. "I recommend that you limit these to no more than five goals, and keep them short and conversational. I've made the mistake of making a goal too long and complicated, and no one could remember it."

"Can you share one of the goals from the professional services firm?" Shauna adjusted the beige-and-maroon silk scarf around her neck.

"Of course. One of our goals was to ensure a fantastic user experience. It was simple and got to the heart of our mission."

"Agreed." Jen pushed a lock of her hair behind her ear. "How did you keep it to five goals? I feel like we could have ten or more."

"Again, not easy, but you have to keep these focused on the key things you want to accomplish. Your goals should also be measurable and memorable. No one can remember ten complicated goals."

"Makes perfect sense." Jen sighed.

"Strategy has to be something unique and different for it to be effective," Meg continued. "This is where creativity really comes in. I encourage you to look for inspiration from outside of the business world."

Shauna and Jen exchanged perplexed glances.

"Okay, I'm having another license-plate moment." Jen shook her head and smiled. "We don't follow."

"Fair enough," Meg acknowledged. "Think about the experiences that leave you with the best memories and feelings. This can be anything from sports teams, clubs, summer camps, schools, places of worship—even your neighborhood Trader Joe's. I mean, c'mon, who doesn't leave Trader Joe's without a smile on their face?"

"Yeah." Shauna's eyes got wide. "I've always had a secret theory that they pump happy gas through the vents there."

"Now, focus in on what makes those experiences unique"— Meg reclined back in her chair—"assuming it's not happy gas. Or maybe we can just pump some through the Dominal facility!"

Jen and Shauna laughed.

"Look, a while back one of my clients was experiencing high first-year turnover and asked me to help them rethink their onboarding. We researched how universities on-board freshmen and set them up for success. We used that model as inspiration and developed a more comprehensive onboarding experience with multiple check-ins to see how the employee was adjusting throughout the year."

"Did it work?" Jen asked.

"Yep. Not only did it cut down on turnover, it also created a much more engaged employee from the start."

"Makes sense. I wonder . . ." Jen tapped her pen on the conference room table. "I went to art camp back in high school. Even though we all went our separate ways, we keep in touch, even all these years later. There was something unique about that experience. I need to think about what that was."

"Any other pearls of wisdom as we start designing, Meg?" Shauna continued to type on her laptop. "I want to hear them all."

"Many!" Meg folded her hands on her desk. "But I'll just give you a few key ones before you dive in. Design from the perspective of the employee and manager. Make your programs and services as intuitive as a cell phone app. Aim to make it so easy that they don't need any training. You want employees and managers to feel compelled to use your programs and services because they want to, not because they have to."

"Interesting," Shauna said. "A whole different approach."

"Actually, it makes a lot of sense," Jen chimed in. "Too often the focus is compliance, not our people. I like that."

"You got it!" Meg smiled. "If the employees see value and feel like they are being treated as people, they'll engage. Okay, guys, I need to go call that Uber to head to my next meeting. Go forth and design! Reach out if you need me."

———◇———

"Whatcha watching?" Jen curled up next to Dave on the dark gray sectional in their family room. It was a cold, dreary Saturday evening, and the roaring flames in the fireplace warmed the room. Jen had just put the kids to bed after some family time at Chuck E. Cheese.

"Just the news." Dave stayed focused on the TV. "Hey, hon, do you think you could handle school drop-off next week? I'm swamped with Tanya's transfer."

"No problem. You've been so great lately, it's the least I can do." Jen tousled his hair. "You doing okay? That's a big change."

Dave frowned and shrugged his shoulders. "I don't know. Part of the reason I joined Advantage was to work with her. She's terrific."

"I know. But you can't blame her. Leading the company's West Coast finance team. San Francisco . . . I mean, that's quite an opportunity."

"Yeah, I get that." Dave mumbled.

"But?"

"I guess . . ." Dave shook his head. "I mean . . . it just won't be the same without her."

"Well, you still get to work with her." Jen turned her face toward him. "She'll still be part of the company."

Dave sat motionless, unwilling to meet her gaze. Jen looped her arm into Dave's and rested her chin on his shoulder. "I can tell there's something else."

Dave grabbed the remote from the side table and muted the TV. "There is. This may sound crazy, but I wonder if I should put my hat in the ring as her replacement."

Jen pulled her head back and faced Dave. "Do you think you're ready?"

Dave threw his hands in the air. "I don't know. I haven't been at the company very long, and it would be a huge learning curve . . . but I have had a few key successes, and I have some experience. I have a meeting with Regina on Tuesday. What do you think?"

Jen though quietly for a few moments. "Well, maybe instead of saying, 'I want to put my hat in the ring,' try something like, 'I'm interested in growing my career here, and I'd like to be considered for Tanya's job . . . but I'm not sure I'm ready.' Tell Regina you've put together some ideas, and ask her if she's willing to talk it through with you."

Dave crossed his arms. "Hmm . . . that may work. This way, I'm not walking into her office sounding entitled. I'm just interested and curious."

"Right, and looking for feedback," Jen replied. "I think that's a much better approach than trying to convince her that you're ready when you're not even sure you are, right?"

"Yeah, I like it." Dave nodded. "I'm going to give it a try. Thanks for your help, hon."

Dave kissed Jen's temple when she reached across him to unmute the TV. A rerun of *Friends* was playing, and they both relaxed and settled in. Once the show was over, Jen turned off the TV and turned toward her husband. "I know it's late, but any chance you were able to take a look at my HR strategy?"

"Yeah, I reviewed it this morning." Dave, avoiding eye contact, focused on Jen's oil painting of Navy Pier, which was hanging on the far wall of the family room. "I don't know what to say, sweetheart."

"You don't like it?" Jen's heart started to race.

"That's not it." Dave turned to face her. "I've just . . . well, I've never seen anything like it. I mean, it's good, fresh, different . . . and totally business focused. It's also thoughtful from a people perspective . . ."

"I sense a 'but' coming." Jen angled her head.

Dave shifted his gaze to the fireplace. "My question is . . . well . . . is it too good to be true?"

"Oh. Ha. That's not what I was expecting." Jen shrugged. "I don't know . . . maybe. According to Meg, it's supposed to be aspirational."

"Oh, you nailed that," Dave interjected, a hint of sarcasm in his tone.

"Buuuut—"Jen rubbed her forehead with her left hand. "Did you like HR's vision?"

"Yeah. I like how you tied HR's vision to fostering innovation. And I thought it was cool how you connected it to both the employees and external stuff that most HR departments don't think about, like consumers and communities."

"Meg encouraged us to be *that* bold," Jen said. "It's definitely a different way of thinking about things."

"Yep." Dave stroked the day-old stubble on his chin. "Okay, but help me understand. How does innovation apply if I'm a finance employee?"

"That's the interesting part." Jen pushed away the few loose hairs that had fallen out of her ponytail. "One of the common themes I heard was that everyone loves that Dominal is always looking for new ways to get things done across every department—finance, R&D, or operations."

"And now HR," Dave added. "I see. So, your HR mission about empowering employees to cultivate their best ideas has a double meaning?"

"Hmm . . . possibly." Jen grinned. "Really, we're just amplifying something everyone already loves about the company."

Dave twiddled his thumbs and sat quietly. Jen sat next to him and studied his expression, trying to figure out what was going on in his head. His feedback was important to her. She knew he would be fair and honest.

"Hold on." Dave got up and walked over to the kitchen. He opened the fridge and pulled out two PBRs.

"Have you really thought about the implications of this?" he asked gently, handing Jen a beer. "I mean, do you think your team can do this?"

"Seriously, Dave, PBR?" Jen pushed away the beer with a smile.

"What? We're out of everything else. One of us needs to hit the store tomorrow."

"There's no way I'm drinking that stuff unless we're watching baseball."

"Suit yourself. More for me." Dave cracked open his beer.

"You may be the only person on the planet that's ever said that about PBR."

"Nah, you know any of my college buddies would agree."

Jen snorted. "Well, that's a *huge* endorsement!"

"Back to the topic at hand." Dave took a sip. "Have you thought about the implications?"

"Yes, way too much. I know I'll have to make some hard decisions over the next few months."

"Will you have Mark's support?"

"Do you mean when I tell him that I'll be letting people go?" Jen shook her head. "I don't know. I'm sure he'll tell me it's my decision, but it's another thing when we're talking about actual people being fired—especially those who've been with Dominal for years."

Dave reached for her hand. She rested her head on his shoulder. "Unfortunately, I don't think you have a choice."

"I know." Jen felt her throat tighten and tears burning along the edges of her eyelids and soaking into Dave's T-shirt. She hadn't cried in front of him in a long time, not even when her parents moved to Florida.

Dave's thumb traced circles on her shoulder.

"Look, you don't have to do this." He murmured. "You could quit. My salary is enough to hold us over—"

"No," Jen interrupted quietly. "Honestly, yes, I'm scared. I've never done anything like this before. But at the same time, it makes so much sense. I've got to believe in myself. I'm not going to give up now."

Dave set his beer down on the side table and put his other arm around her and pulled her closer. "Look, Mark brought in Meg to help you come up with something bold. That's what you're doing."

"Are you just saying that to make me feel better?"

Dave pulled back and looked Jen straight in the eye. "No, I mean it. This is a real opportunity for you and your team."

"Thanks." Jen exhaled and cast her eyes on Kat's favorite toy, which had been left next to the couch. "It's hard, but if we don't make bold changes now, we won't be competitive. It'd be a disaster."

———⊰⊱———

Jen was startled by the soft knock at her office door late Tuesday afternoon.

"Sorry, didn't mean to scare you, Jen." Mark was standing in her office doorway. "Do you have a minute?"

"Sure. Come in." Jen motioned toward the guest chairs. "Just catching up on the sinkhole that is my inbox."

"Ha, I understand." Mark shut the door and made his way to the chair. "I just stopped by Shauna's office to thank her for all of her effort on the HR strategy."

"Thanks, Mark." Jen smiled broadly. "I'm sure she was delighted to get a personal thank-you from you. Very nice of you."

"My pleasure." Mark folded his hands in his lap. "Your team did a great job, and I wanted to personally thank you too."

"Thanks, it was a team effort." Jen relaxed back in her chair. "Everyone contributed, and Meg really pushed our thinking on this. I couldn't have done it without her and Shauna."

There was another soft knock at the door.

"Hey, guys." Allan opened Jen's door. "Am I interrupting?"

"Not at all." Mark smiled. "I'm sure you're here for the same reason I am."

"Yeah." Allan stepped in and propped one shoulder against the wall. "Great work, Jen. I mean, Rich was speechless! I'm not sure I've ever seen that before."

"And I'm not sure we'll see it again!" Jen chimed in.

The three colleagues laughed.

"What's so funny?" Michelle popped her head in the doorway.

"Oh, nothing. We were just commenting on Rich's reaction to the new HR strategy." Jen motioned for Michelle to sit in the guest chair next to Mark.

"You really think I'm going to sit down?" Michelle shook her head and made her way to the back corner of the office. "In all seriousness, I'm really excited. It's so energizing, so different."

"I keep thinking about the focus on innovation," Allan added. "I know my team will love that."

"Yeah, especially the new head of R&D." Mark sat forward in his chair. "It looks like that external search firm you hired has some good candidates lined up. I'm sure we'll be mentioning the new strategy in interviews."

"Am I missing a meeting?" The group looked up to see Rich just outside Jen's doorway.

"No, everyone just wandered in." Mark gestured for Rich to enter. "Come in, Rich."

Allan moved further into Jen's office and sat on her credenza to make room for Rich.

"So, what's going on?" Rich smacked on his chewing gum. "Are we plotting to take over the world?"

"Perhaps tomorrow, Richie Rich!" Allan teased. "Today, we're talking about Jen's new strategy."

"Ah! Yeah, good work." Rich glanced at Jen. "I like the direction, but is it really possible?"

"It's got to work. We don't have a choice if we're going to meet our six-month targets." Mark adjusted his glasses and turned from Rich toward Jen. "I forgot to ask earlier, how will you measure your success? I don't recall seeing any metrics."

"That's a great question, Mark." Jen smiled confidently. "I'm on it. Just give me until next week."

CHAPTER 8

"SO, IT WAS *really* cool that Mark stopped by to personally thank me." Shauna took a sip of her tequila late afternoon on a Thursday.

"You totally deserve it. You both did a great job on the strategy—and we *all* deserve a little break from the constant pressure of those six-month targets!" Michelle lifted her stein of Coors Light and took a big gulp. "Boy, that hits the spot!"

"I can't believe you drink that stuff!" Jen shook her head. "Dave tried to get me to drink a PBR last Saturday, and I let him know in no uncertain terms would that happen outside of a baseball setting."

"It's from all the years of hanging out with the ops guys. I developed a taste for it. Trust me, I would have never won their respect drinking anything but cheap beer. Plus, I don't know how you try to drink anything other than cheap beer at a place like this." Michelle side-eyed Jen and Shauna.

Jen glanced around the worn gray walls of the busy bar they frequented around the corner from Dominal's headquarters. It was an easy walk, with most of it sheltered from the wind and harsh weather, which also meant it was a local favorite. "This place amazes me. I mean, I get there's nowhere else to go within a five-mile radius, but I was just thinking they haven't done anything to this place since, like, 1990."

"I'm just glad we got a booth today." Shauna rolled up the sleeves of her light pink button-down. She studied the group of people gathering at the bar. "It's so hard to believe how crowded this place gets."

"By the way"—Jen raised her head, scanned the bar for anyone she might recognize, and then lowered her voice—"did you know Rich is a White Sox fan?"

"No way!" Michelle laughed. "Somehow I'm not surprised."

"He can't be the only one at Dominal." Shauna swirled her tequila in her glass. "But they do keep pretty quiet."

"Yeah, Dominal is a Cubs company first!" Jen replied.

"Except it's led by a Red Sox fan!" Michelle interjected. "I get that Mark is from Boston, but at some point you have to give in and cheer for the Cubs!"

Shauna and Jen laughed. The revolving doors of the bar kept turning, ushering in more and more people, and the noise level seemed to go up a notch every few minutes.

"So, what's next, you two?" Michelle put her schooner down with a slight thud on the scratched wooden table. "How are you going to move forward with the strategy?"

"Well, I think we need to start aligning the team and get to those success metrics I mentioned." Jen played with her cocktail napkin. "We're also meeting with the HR team on Monday to start thinking through how this impacts their day-to-day work, and then I have a meeting with Meg next Wednesday to—oh, shoot! I just remembered, I have that all-day FMLA briefing and will be out of the office. I guess I need to reschedule with Meg and let Mark know I won't have the metrics until the following week."

"You're going to the full-day briefing?" Shauna gave Jen a bemused look.

"Yeah, I go every year. Gotta keep sharp on the compliance stuff too!" Jen tapped the side of her head and smiled. She pulled out her phone to quickly text Meg and Mark.

"I'm going to go grab some pretzels from the bar." Michelle jumped up. "Anyone need anything?"

Jen and Shauna shook their heads. Michelle pushed her way through the gathering crowd at the bar until her black sweater and dark jeans blended into the crowd fully, and she disappeared from sight.

"That woman can't sit still for five minutes!" Shauna observed. "How does she handle meetings?"

"Everyone knows she has to keep moving." Jen leaned forward to take off her charcoal pinstripe blazer. She folded it neatly next to her and sat back in her silver silk shirt. "She takes laps around the boardroom during leadership team meetings. I actually think Mark is amused by it. I give her credit, though, she never misses a beat."

"Interesting." Shauna shook her head. "I guess whatever works!"

A few minutes later, Michelle re-emerged from the crowd and dropped a bowl of pretzels in the center of the table. "Dang, this place is becoming a madhouse! So, FMLA? That's family leave?"

"Yep—it's a pretty big overhaul." Shauna sipped her tequila. "Michelle, what are you up to the rest of the night?"

"I promised Joe I would take care of dinner tonight." Michelle took a sip of beer. "Little does he know that just means I'll pick up pizza on the way home. Good thing we're working out tomorrow morning! We've been eating like crap the last month. What about you?"

"Yeah, it's been crazy." Shauna gazed up. "Ravi and I are doing a date night. I haven't really been able to spend time with him these past few weeks, so I'm excited."

"That's still going well?" Michelle asked.

"Yeah, eighteen months." Shauna smiled and crossed her fingers. "And no red flags yet!"

"Awesome! I've really liked him the few times I've met him." Michelle wiped the condensation from her beer mug. "Jen, what about you?"

"Well, that's odd." Jen stared at her phone. "I just texted Meg about rescheduling and asked her if she was planning to attend the one in California, and she replied that she is not planning to attend any briefings."

"Maybe she's super busy with client work?" Shauna offered.

"Yeah, maybe. I'm just surprised, given what she does and how significant these changes are." Jen put her phone away and picked up her near-empty wine glass. "Sorry, Michelle, what were you asking?"

"Just if you were doing anything tonight." Michelle sipped her beer. "Shauna and Ravi are going out on a date."

"Oh, life before kids!" Jen took a sip of wine. "Nope, we'll probably do our usual: attempt to watch an hour of Netflix and fall asleep on the couch ten minutes in!"

The three of them shook their heads and laughed.

The following morning, Shauna looked up from her tablet and focused her gaze on Jen, who was dressed in a navy suit with a tan blouse and seated at her desk. Shauna had just briefed Jen on a complicated benefits issue and had something else on her mind.

"Can I ask you something?"

"Of course." Jen closed her file folder. "You know you can ask me anything. What's up?"

"Well, it's just that we have a benefits administrator on our team who handles leave of absence and FMLA. Why are you going to a full-day briefing on this topic?"

"That's a good question." Jen twirled her hair. "I've been thinking about this a bit today. I just feel like they administer the policies, but it's my job to guide them."

"Really?" Shauna sat back in her chair and pulled back her fitted, light yellow knit sweater. "I kinda think it's *my* job to guide them, as their manager."

"Oh, yes, it definitely is." Jen tipped forward. "I'm not suggesting anything else."

Shauna tilted her head. "So, I'm still confused as to why you're going to this briefing?"

"Well, you know, I think the leadership team still expects me to be the HR legal and compliance expert at the company." Jen sat back in her chair. "I need to have a good grasp of the details on this. There are a lot of changes."

Shauna was quiet, trying to understand Jen's perspective. Shauna wanted to be respectful of her boss, but she was struggling to understand how Jen attending the briefing advanced the strategy they had spent so much time working on these past few weeks.

"Are you sure?" Shauna asked softly. "I mean, that's not how you positioned HR in the new strategy. We don't say we're compliance or legal experts."

"Of course we don't say that. Meg told us our strategy isn't about keeping the lights on. But that doesn't mean we don't still have to make sure that stuff gets done," Jen said with a hint of irritation. "Would *you* rather go to the legal briefing?"

"No, but with all due respect," Shauna began, straightening up in her chair, "I'm too focused on the other things you've assigned me as part of our new strategy."

"I agree, and I want you to stay focused on the strategy. One of us needs to go, so it should be me." Jen tapped her pen on the desk.

"Okay, then." Shauna stood up to leave. "Well, let me know if there's stuff we need to share with the team."

"I'm just not sure about what to do." Jen flipped the switch to turn off the can lights in their master bathroom before heading back to her laptop, which she'd left on her side of their king-size bed. The temperature was in the low twenties, and despite all the work they had done to improve the insulation in the house the past summer, there was still a slight draft. Jen had just changed into her flannel pajamas and thick sleep socks. She shivered as she pulled back the beige comforter and climbed into the warm bed.

"Personally, I'd be poking my eyes out if I had to listen to an attorney spew on about FMLA law." Dave looked up from his laptop and rolled his eyes. "Actually, I'd have the same re-action if I had to listen to an attorney spew on about anything for longer than an hour!"

Jen focused on her screen. "But I've heard you talk about going to briefings on accounting principles."

"Have I?" Dave looked up at the smooth, white ceiling. "I mean, I guess I have to know the big picture stuff, so yeah—*maybe* a short briefing every now and then, but the detailed ones I leave to our accounting team."

"Yeah, I've been wondering if I'm thinking about this all wrong. I think I should be approaching HR the same way finance approaches its function—it's the only way we can have the impact we need." Jen shook her head. "And I keep going back to compliance conversations with the leadership team. I mean, are they expecting me to know the details of everything, or am I putting this expectation on myself?"

"That's a good question. If it helps you, in finance, I think I'm expected to be aware of things, but not an expert on the details. Even our accounting team gets outside help when they deal with really technical issues." Dave turned off his computer.

"Yeah, that helps." Jen sighed. "I know I have to be strategic, and with these aggressive board targets, maybe this isn't where I should be spending my time."

"I think you're thinking about it the right way." Dave put his laptop on the dresser, crawled under the covers, and kissed Jen on the cheek. "Sleep on it and see how you feel in the morning. I'm going to hit the sack. Good night."

"Yeah, it's late, and I'm sure our favorite alarm will visit us early." Jen smiled at the thought of Cooper and Kat climbing into bed with them for a few minutes in the morning. "Good night."

"Umm . . . Shauna?" Jen stood a few feet behind Shauna in the deserted break room.

Shauna turned around. "Oh, hey, I was just grabbing some green tea."

"Me too." Jen held up her empty mug. "Hey, about earlier, I owe you an apology. I thought about what you said, and it doesn't make sense for either of us to go to that legal briefing. We should be focused on the strategic stuff, like you pointed out."

"Oh, good." Shauna smiled and moved away from the hot water machine. "I'm glad to hear it."

"I've asked Elena Lopez of Kasper & Hanson to schedule an hour with us and the benefits team next week to get a high-level summary of the changes. We can figure out next steps from there."

"That sounds like a plan." Shauna sipped her tea. "Say, do you have a minute to go back to my office? I want to show you this new technology I'm looking at. It could really help us automate some of the benefits stuff."

"Ugh, I really want to," Jen said, pouring hot water into her mug, "but I really need to focus on the strategy metrics. Can I take a rain check?"

"Of course. I'll put some time on your calendar."

"Great!" Jen smiled. "I look forward to it."

Shauna turned around and nearly collided with Mark, who was standing at the entrance of the break room. "Oh, sorry, Mark!"

"You're good, Shauna." Mark took a few steps back. "Leanne always tells me to stop creeping up behind people. I guess I never learn. How are you doing?"

"Great!" Shauna exclaimed. "I am actually off to go meet with my team to discuss some details of our strategy implementation."

"Love it." Mark smiled as she left and headed back to her office.

"So, Jen. Back to green tea?"

"Yeah, I'm doing a detox." Jen stepped to the side to make room for Mark at the counter. "I need to get back to being healthy."

"Yeah, it's been a tough few weeks. I'm looking forward to getting back to my regular exercise routine." Mark pulled out a clean mug from the cabinet and began filling it with hot water. "I got your note. What changed your mind about the legal briefing?"

"You know, I just realized that part of my job is to rely on experts." Jen steeped her tea bag. "And in order for us to execute this strategy and get Dominal back on track, I have to focus on the best use of my time. A day-long briefing doesn't make sense."

"Good." Mark smiled and pulled out a tea bag. "I'd agree. We'll always invest in legal counsel when needed—this is a commitment from our board and a key principle in how we manage our risk."

"Makes sense."

"So . . ." Mark unwrapped a tea bag. "How are you feeling about the Cubs this year? I know how *excited* you and Michelle get during the postseason."

"You know," Jen got excited, "if our pitching is as strong as it was the other day, I think we have a real chance. And for the record, I'm nowhere near as obsessed as Michelle."

"Come on, Jen." Mark shook his head and steeped his tea. "Last year, both of you 'worked from home' after they lost the NL championship."

"Look, Mark, it's stressful being a Cubs fan." Jen blew the steam away from her tea. "Michelle even has a shirt that says, 'I can't stay calm, I'm a Cubs fan'!"

Mark chuckled. "You know, pitching alone can't earn them a spot in the World Series. How will you beat the Dodgers? They've really come together as a team and are firing on all cylinders. The Cubs have such little offense right now."

"Our hitting will come back." Jen threw out her tea bag. "We were just off the other day."

"I'll believe it when I see it." Mark rolled his eyes. "They seem unfocused. One week it's the hitting, the next it's the pitching. The Dodgers are consistent."

"We may have had a few slipups recently, but don't count us out. We'll regroup and come back stronger than ever." Jen sipped her tea. "What about you? How're you feeling about the Red Sox?"

"Pretty good!" Mark steeped his tea. "I think we'll be hard to beat."

"What about the Astros? Aren't you worried about them?"

"A little," Mark admitted. "I mean, it'll be tough, but I think if we play like we've been playing, we can beat them."

"A word of advice." Jen angled her head, lowered her voice, and gave a mischievous smile. "If it comes down to the Red Sox and the Cubs in the World Series, I'd take a two-week vacation if I were you. Dominal is Cubs territory, no matter who its leader is."

CHAPTER 9

"GO AHEAD." MEG rolled up the sleeves of her blue chambray shirt during their Zoom call the next Thursday morning. "I know you want to talk about it."

"So . . ." Jen nodded excitedly from her office. "You watched the game?"

"No." Meg took a sip of her water. "But I got a text this morning from my friend, and I know how you Cubs fans get."

"It was amazing! Awesome! I can't wait for tomorrow night. I know we still have a long way to go, but I feel good . . . *really* good." Jen straightened up in her chair and took a deep breath. "I'll stop since you already got the details."

"I'm happy for you and will silently cheer for the Cubs." Meg smiled. "Unless, of course, you're up against the Dodgers. I have to stay true to my LA roots, even if I am not really a baseball fan."

"Fine, whatever," Jen said with a sigh. "Why'd you have to piss in my Cheerios?"

"What?" Meg put her hand to her mouth to stop herself from spitting water on the screen. "Where did *that* come from?"

"Sorry." Jen chuckled. "I guess my baseball vocabulary may not be appropriate for work."

"No, no." Meg shook her head as she wiped water from her lips. "It's fine . . . it's just that I wasn't expecting that from you. But don't get me wrong, I like it. May even borrow it."

"Have at it." Jen smiled. "Dave and I used to say stuff like that all the time before we had kids. Now we're worried that we'll get a call from school about one of them parroting our colorful language, so we've pared back."

"Smart." Meg laughed. "Ready to get started?"

"Yes." Jen sipped green tea from her *#1 Mom* mug. "I started working on the success metrics. Let me share my screen."

Jen maneuvered her mouse to share her slides. Meg leaned toward her monitor to get a closer look and scrunched her face while she processed them.

"Interesting." Meg rubbed her hands together. "These are good. I like the categories of engagement, productivity, and retention."

"Yeah, those felt to me like they really addressed our key gaps right now without using HR jargon, like we've talked about."

"Yep, for sure. I also like that you kept it to just a handful of metrics that all tie into business outcomes, and you've included the Glassdoor ratings." Meg picked up her Slinky and stretched it. "But I feel like something is missing here."

"Missing?"

"Okay, Jen, let's say that you achieve these metrics, and the business doesn't meet its goals." Meg put her Slinky down. "Is your strategy still a success?"

"I'm not following." Jen exhaled deeply.

"Well, you *are* part of the leadership team." Meg tapped her chin. "So that means that you're held accountable for the company's success, just like everyone else, right?"

"Yes . . ." Jen took a sip of green tea.

"So, where are Dominal's business performance metrics? You have to show that you have skin in the game, just like everyone else."

"I do have skin in the game. Productivity and retention are both tied to sales and profitability," Jen argued. "Without these, there's no way we can meet our business goals."

"Hmm . . . let me ask you another question. At our first meeting, you talked about the 2016 World Series."

"Okay, I love this question already," Jen said, relaxing. "Clearly. It's one of my absolute favorite Series of all time."

"So, what if the Cubs had the best pitching lineup ever? The pitchers did everything one hundred percent right. Maybe even one hundred and *ten* percent right." Meg looked Jen right in the eye. "But they couldn't get their offense or defense working, and the Cubs ended up losing to Cleveland. Would they still be World Series champs?"

"What? No, that's ridiculous." Jen shook her head. "Seriously, Meg, how do you come up with this stuff?"

"I didn't come up with it." Meg chuckled. "You did. But you were talking about HR instead of the Cubs."

Jen looked away from the screen and gazed at the red squiggly lines of her office's abstract art while she thought about what Meg said. After a few moments, she exhaled loudly. "Ugh. Okay, I see it now. The HR strategy can only be a success if Dominal achieves its business goals."

"Right." Meg leaned back in her chair. "Dominal's business performance is the ultimate goal here. Without it, you don't win the game."

"Okay, I'll add some success metrics." Jen jotted down some notes. "Anything else?"

"I think it looks good." Meg bit her bottom lip. "But I want to stick with baseball for a minute. You know, I am always fascinated at how the coaches make decisions. Why do they change pitchers so often?"

"It's a data-driven approach." Jen gestured with her hands in excitement. "There's a team of analysts that crunch data from the past, and they model it to make decisions about the future. The analytics actually tell them exactly when to replace the pitcher for the greatest chance of winning the game."

"Okay, you can put your arms down now. You're very passionate about baseball, aren't you?" Meg grinned.

"I'm especially excitable postseason." Jen laughed. "But seriously, why did you ask me that?"

"First, I'm just curious because my friends start yelling at the coach to change or not change the pitcher, but the coach never budges. Baffles me. If it weren't for the beer and Dodger dogs, I probably wouldn't ever bother with baseball."

Jen laughed. "And second?"

"Well . . ." Meg clasped her hands. "I'd like you to think about how you can apply data in a similar way to make HR decisions."

"What do you mean?" Jen turned the page in her moleskin notebook.

"One of the main reasons HR struggles with leadership is it often relies on anecdotes rather than data to make decisions." Meg folded her hands on the desk. "I mean, think about it, Jen—would a CEO agree to pay a stock dividend or invest in a new market without an analysis of internal and external data to make sure it made sense?"

"That's not a fair comparison. It's hard to apply data to people," Jen countered. "People are so . . . unpredictable."

"And yet they've figured out how to do it in baseball?" Meg cocked her head. "How is that different?"

"Uh, well." Jen was stunned. "I, um . . . never thought about it that way."

"That's okay," Meg acknowledged. "This is tough for companies to absorb. Less than fifteen percent of companies use analytics to make people decisions."

"Wow!" Jen jerked her head back slightly. "Sounds like it's an opportunity to get ahead of our talent challenges. But where would I even get started? I mean, I'm not even sure we have all the data we'd need."

"Start with what you have. You'll never have a complete set of data, but what group does? Sales and marketing have to make decisions based on a subset of data—why can't HR do the same thing?"

"That's true." Jen's eyes focused on the drop ceiling. "I mean, something is better than nothing."

"There are some ways to experiment with this." Meg leaned forward in her chair. "When I was leading talent acquisition, we evaluated external economic measures and how the changes impacted talent trends. You know, things like changes in GDP, unemployment. We used this information to look for correlations."

"Did you find any?"

"Actually, yes. We figured out that an increase in GDP typically meant an increase in our recruiting and retention costs." Meg straightened up in her chair. "We could then look at GDP forecasts for future years and be proactive about what we needed to do be successful."

"That's cool! I love that, Meg. It's a simple concept, but probably hard to model."

"Yeah, we had finance help. They were more than willing to do it because they didn't like surprises either."

Jen sat on the edge of her chair. "Maybe you and I can get together with Allan to discuss further? I think we could use your help on this."

"Love to. It's one of my favorite areas to dig into." Meg smiled. "Okay, my friend, time to run to my next meeting. Talk soon!"

A week later the team gathered in Allan's office to discuss their first draft of the data analysis the team had put together. Outside Allan's office window, Jen's eye caught the visible mounds of snow in the parking lot and the street that had accumulated during the prior evening's storm and briefly wondered if her kids were going sledding after school.

"Wow, this is great." Mark spoke to the Polycom centered on the small conference table in Allan's office and refocused Jen back on the matter at hand. "We do this in other areas of our business to get ahead of trends. Awesome seeing it applied to HR as well."

"Yeah, there hasn't been a lot of traction around using analytics to predict talent trends." Meg's voice echoed through the speakers. "And you're just scratching the surface with what you can do. Could become a real competitive advantage for you."

"Exactly. GDP was a good start," Jen chimed in. "I knew a booming economy impacted recruiting, but now we know how much it does and can get ahead of it."

Allan shut his laptop and walked the short distance back to his desk. "The finance team is ready to do all kinds of sophisticated data analyses to figure out what else they can model and learn about HR. I personally am really excited for this challenge and where it can take us."

"Let's present this to Michelle and Rich at our next leadership meeting." Mark stood up from his chair. "Thanks for your help with all this, Meg. We'll talk soon."

"Sure, guys. Take care."

Mark and Jen walked out of Allan's office together and headed toward Jen's office. Mark followed Jen in and closed the door behind them.

"Just wanted to say—really good work, Jen."

"Thanks." Jen made her way to her desk and put her papers down. "You know, it's weird, Allan was really engaged, which was great—but I still have this nagging feeling the leadership team isn't fully on board yet."

Mark gave her a puzzled look. "What do you mean?"

"I just get this sense that there's still some uncertainty." Jen sat down at her desk. "Like, it's good on paper, but they don't believe my team can really do this."

"The leadership team is excited, they said it themselves. They just need to see some results. There's a lot on the line here, and you're proposing a whole new way of getting things done."

"I guess." Jen rubbed her temples.

"Remember, this is just the first step." Mark reclined in the office chair. "And it's a big one. You know you're going to have to really get your team aligned and executing against it. That's another big lift. And we both know that you've got some people on the team who won't be able to make the transition. They're just too stuck in their old ways."

"Yeah, I've been thinking about that a lot lately." Jen leaned her head back and closed her eyes. "It's going to be a tough few months."

"Look, you can't afford to wait too long on staff changes," Mark cautioned. "Everyone's going to be watching to see what you do over these next few months and how quickly you take action when people won't adapt."

"I know," Jen said softly. "Ugh, it's just something I'll never ever get used to."

"It's hard, but the biggest mistakes I've made in my career, even at Davis & Edwards, were always about not taking swift action with people when I knew things weren't going to change." Mark sighed. "My leadership team was frustrated with my performance. My colleagues were frustrated watching me put up with the dysfunction. Heck, I was frustrated with myself."

Jen exhaled. "Yeah, Shauna's already getting pushback from some of her team."

"Have the talk with her too," Mark advised. "I don't want Shauna to lose enthusiasm because she's fighting an uphill battle. You should have a plan to take quick action. We will do the right thing with severance. I have a feeling some of our long-time employees are going to be impacted."

"Thanks, Mark." Jen looked at him and smiled. "Your support means a lot."

"You have it completely. Let's keep the momentum going." Mark stood up to leave. "Speaking of momentum, did you see my team last night? We were on fire."

"Whatever." Jen put her hand up to him. "Boston still has to beat the Astros before they can make it to the World Series. I wish you luck, but you know it's never gonna happen!"

"Ah, grasshopper, you have such little faith. Don't count us out!" Mark winked and left Jen's office.

CHAPTER 10

"I'M ENCOURAGED THAT our action plans look like they're start-ing to work." Mark stood in front of the leadership team on a Monday morning. "Early indications show that we're on track to meet the six-month targets. We still have a ton of work to do, and we can't take our eye off the ball, but so far, so good."

The leadership team had gathered in the boardroom for their weekly meeting to review the progress and discuss actions and bot-tlenecks key to driving their plan forward. Jen noticed that Mark seemed to have more confidence than he'd had in a long while.

"That's great news." Michelle stood up into the bright morn-ing sun that was streaming into the conference room. "Do you think the board feels the same way?"

"I had dinner with Renata last night, and they are cautiously optimistic." Mark cleaned his glasses. "They are meeting with our final R&D leader candidate tomorrow, so hopefully we can wrap that up soon. It will be a huge win for us."

Jen sat up at the mention of the R&D search. She was pleased that the recruiting firm she brought in was making such terrific progress. "I think Juanita will be a terrific addition to the team."

"For sure." Mark opened a folder and pulled out a report. "Okay, I want to address turnover. The ops numbers are looking better thanks to our focus there, but—"

"I know, I know," Rich interjected. "You're going to bring up sales turnover. I feel the pain every day, but I'm working on it."

"What's going on there, Rich?" Mark stroked his chin. "We need to get on top of this as soon as possible, as this is one of those things that could derail us if we don't stop the bleeding. Have you and Jen dug into this?"

"Well . . ." Rich gave a satisfied smile. "I just signed up a new software vendor that will give us real-time feedback with an app that works with our existing tools."

"Cool!" Michelle's blue eyes brightened. "What does it do?"

"It uses artificial intelligence and asks our employees questions on their cell phones or through email. Then it summarizes how everyone on the team is feeling about their work. This information gets stored in a data warehouse, so the system can build analytics and help us understand trends better over time." Rich flipped his tablet to show the team a brightly colored dashboard filled with graphs and charts. "I can monitor and change reports as needed."

"What program is this?" Jen could feel her muscles tensing underneath her pale blue pantsuit. "I'm not sure I've heard anything about a pilot."

"SeeMe." Rich turned his tablet around, but kept his gaze on the screen, not Jen.

"Oh, right," Jen chimed in, "the sales rep kept calling me, but I didn't pursue it. Tight budget, as you well know. How did you get the money for it?"

"It's a pilot. Dirt cheap. No commitments." Rich looked over at Allan. "And if we like it, I know we'll figure out a way to pay for it."

"If it helps us get ahead on turnover"—Allan stood up from the table to refill his coffee mug —"I *know* we can find the money."

Jen took a deep, calming breath. "Look, Rich, you can't just roll these things out without talking to me. You have to give me a heads-up. HR needs to be involved."

"Jen, you never even returned the rep's calls," Rich replied, his voice slightly raised. "And I don't want your team mucking this up. HR slows down everything. We're moving forward with the pilot. I have a real engagement problem and need to figure out what's happening."

"C'mon, Rich, you know we're working on an engagement survey to diagnose what's happening in a broader way." Jen glared directly into Rich's eyes. "This is going to cause confusion."

"The engagement survey is taking too long. It's time to shake things up. We need to think differently." Rich turned to Mark.

"This guy told me he's been trying to break into our company for months. I need help right now, and I looked at this demo and couldn't figure out why HR refused to take the guy's call."

Allan and Michelle exchanged knowing glances. No one was surprised that Rich was a lone wolf and a rebel; he had a reputation throughout the company for doing what he needed to get done and not wanting to play by anyone else's rules.

"Okay." Mark's splayed hands moved up and down in the air. "Let's all just calm down."

"We are—*I am* really struggling." Rich shook his head. "And I gotta get a handle on this quickly. I can't wait for HR to get their crap together."

"Okay, but you should've had Jen sit in on the demo," Mark admonished. "We have to support each other; we're not going to meet these aggressive goals unless we work together."

Rich sighed loudly.

"I'm happy to take a look at the software, Rich." Jen gave a tense smile to mask her frustration. "Let's find a time after the meeting."

"I'm still just pissed!" Jen slammed her laptop shut, and Dave watched her pace around their bedroom. "How could he have gone behind my back like that?"

"Yeah, what Rich did was unfair." Dave sat cross-legged on the bed in his white-and-blue plaid pajama bottoms and ragged Cubs sweatshirt. "At a minimum, he should have brought you in right after the demo or given you a heads-up before the meeting."

"You know, it doesn't matter what I do." Jen frowned. "I'm still not treated as an equal."

"Mark defended you in the meeting, right?"

"That's not the point," Jen snapped. "I had a plan to fix this, Dave. It's not like I wasn't working on it. The engagement survey is ready. It's being rolled out in two weeks."

"Honey, c'mon, stay calm," Dave pleaded. "You're gonna wake the kids."

Jen rolled her eyes.

"Can you please stop pacing for a minute? You're wearing out the carpet!" Dave stood up. "Look, Jen, don't take this the wrong way, but Rich has a problem he needs to solve fast. He's accountable for his team's performance."

"I would have helped him!" Jen stopped pacing and faced her husband. "That's my job."

"But you said yourself that you didn't look at the software when they reached out."

"Not helping, *David*!" Jen resumed pacing. "You're supposed to be on my side."

"Jen." Dave put his hands on her shoulders and turned her toward him. "I *am* on your side, but I'm not going to let you play the victim. You're better than that."

Jen sighed.

"You're making progress. You said it yourself." Dave slowly turned Jen so he could massage her shoulders. "But honestly, honey . . ."

Kat began wailing from down the hall.

Dave and Jen raced out of the room, past the kids' bathroom and the family photos that adorned the long hallway until they reached the doorway of the kids' room. Jen reached Kat first, who was sitting up in bed, soaked in tears.

"What's the matter, Kitty Kat?" Jen cradled her little girl in her arms. Dave placed his hand on Kat's forehead.

"She's burning hot," Dave whispered. "I'll go get the thermometer."

———————

"Hey, Meg." Jen sat at her dining room table the next morning. The room was dimly lit.

"What's up?" Meg smiled. "You don't look too sprightly this morning."

"I'm okay." Jen took a sip of coffee. "I'm home today. I was up all night with Kat. High fever. Cooper woke up with one this morning too. I'm exhausted."

"Oh, sorry. That's rough." Meg placed her hand on the side of her face. "Do you still want to talk? We can reschedule."

"No, let's talk. I have a lot on my mind." Jen rubbed her forehead with her left hand. "My in-laws came over first thing this morning to help out, so I have a few hours."

"Good." Meg nodded. "Do you think it's the flu or something else?"

"Not sure." Jen pulled gently on her ponytail, and her eye caught a scratch on the paint, likely the result of Cooper ramming his toy trucks into the wall. "Kat points at her ears and throat when I ask her what hurts."

"I'm glad you could stay home with them. Nothing beats having your mom take care of you when you're not feeling well. And it's nice that you have your in-laws to help."

"Yeah, they're great. It's just . . ." Jen glanced behind her at the oak staircase to make sure no one was within earshot. She whispered, "Well, they're not *my* parents. My dad is a retired pediatrician. He knows how to calm the kids down and make this all better."

"You know, video works wonders," Meg said gently. "You could reach out to them."

"You're right." Jen wiped away a tear. "It's just not the same."

"I get it," Meg rested her chin lightly on her fingers. "Is everything else alright?"

"It's just . . ." Jen started tearing up. "Give me a moment, please."

"Take your time." Meg sat back in her chair. "I'm not going anywhere."

Jen closed her eyes and took a deep breath. She grabbed a tissue and cleaned her face.

"Sorry, Meg." Jen swallowed. "I'm just really tired."

"No need to apologize." Meg folded her hands on her desk. "I'm here if you want to talk."

Jen recounted Rich's behavior at the meeting.

"His approach left a lot to be desired," Meg agreed. "Did you know he was struggling with engagement?"

"Yes, I did." Jen took a sip of coffee. "I mean, it isn't as bad as ops, which is where we've been focused, but it seems to have crept up recently."

"What was your plan for sales?"

"Well, I mean, there are pockets of turnover challenges across the business," Jen acknowledged. "That's why I want to get this engagement survey out. It will uncover sentiment throughout the organization. We want to start doing it every year and then build an action plan."

"Okay." Meg smoothed her light yellow cardigan. "And what are you doing to help Rich now . . . today?"

"I don't know," Jen sighed and looked up at the smooth, white ceiling for a moment. "Okay, help me understand what I could have done differently."

"Well . . . let's start with why you didn't take the software vendor's call."

"Do you know how many calls I get from vendors who claim they can solve all of my problems?" Jen focused her gaze back on the screen. "I don't have the time to listen to each and every one! I'd never get any work done."

"I know it can be overwhelming," Meg agreed, "but Dominal's been struggling with turnover since you joined. It's a major pain point, and this vendor had a solution. Why didn't you listen?"

"Honestly, Meg . . ." Jen exhaled deeply. "I'm not making excuses; I just didn't have time."

"So, speaking of getting inundated with calls," Meg's eyes widened, "I have the same problem with HR technology vendors. Do you know why?"

Jen shook her head.

"They all tell me they don't know how to sell HR," Meg continued. "They want advice. Most vendors stop going to HR; they get no traction, so they go directly to the person who's feeling the most pain."

"Like what SeeMe did," Jen pouted.

"Yes. And the problem is, HR looks reactive every time. Like they're not interested in new ways to solve big problems." Meg took a sip of water. "That's why I advise clients to consider blocking off time on their calendar to make a regular effort to meet with these vendors."

Jen sat quietly for a few moments, contemplating Meg's statement. "Sorry, I'm not trying to be difficult, but that's not the right approach for us in this situation."

"Okay, tell me more," Meg replied.

"I agree that evaluating these technologies is important. But just blocking off time on the calendar will make it a check-the-box kind of activity, and that's not going to drive real change. We must fundamentally rethink how we use technology. It's a mindset change across HR and the company, and I need to lead it," Jen rubbed her temples. "To start with, it will require a more comprehensive and systematic process to evaluate the constant stream of new technologies."

"Fair." Meg smiled. "What are you thinking?"

Jen collected her thoughts. "I think Shauna would really love this. She's always trying to show me new technologies. What if we built a cross-functional taskforce and she leads it? We could also include someone from IT to help evaluate."

"I like where you're going—"

Meg was cut off by Kat's sudden shrieking.

"Ugh. Motrin has worn off." Jen dropped her head in her hands. "I better go."

"Understood. Hope the kids feel better soon." Meg waved as she signed off. "Keep me posted."

"Hi! I can't believe I haven't seen you at all this morning." Shauna stood in Jen's doorway just before eleven fifteen two days later. It was her first day back in the office after being home with the sick kids. "You doing okay?"

"Yeah." Jen looked up from her desk, still exhausted from the last few days. "I've been heads-down today trying to catch up."

"How are the kids?" Shauna tilted her head.

"Better." Jen replied. "They've been fever free for twenty-four hours, but they're still lethargic, so we've kept them home from school. My in-laws are with them."

"Glad their fevers are gone." Shauna took a small step into Jen's office. "I know you're probably slammed, but wanted to check to see if you'd like to grab a quick lunch. I thought it'd be nice to get outside for a bit since the weather's good for a change. If not, can I bring you back something?"

"You know, I could use a break." Jen grabbed her purse. "Let's go."

The weather had made a pleasant turn, and it was in the high sixties when Jen and Shauna stepped out of the office doors. They turned right out and walked at a leisurely place down the empty street, making small talk about the kids and work. They headed toward a small cluster of eateries at the end of the block that catered to the industrial workers in the neighborhood. Even though the streets were empty of people and cars, there was a low humming noise from the various manufacturing taking place in the neighborhood.

"Wow, I didn't realize how nice it was today." Jen took off her tan suit jacket and folded it across her arm.

"Yeah, that's why I wanted to eat outside. We have to make the most of these days when we have them." Shauna gently pushed away the brown hair blowing in her face. "Should we go to the deli?"

"Perfect!" Jen exclaimed. "I am craving one of their wraps."

"I think I'm going to try their new spicy turkey wrap," Shauna said. "Michelle said it was really good."

"Okay, but let's be clear—Michelle thinks Coors Light tastes good." Jen laughed. "So, not sure I trust her opinion on food and drink."

"Good point!"

Clutching their food in brown bags, they exited the deli and turned right. They continued walking about a quarter of a mile down a narrow one-way street until they reached a small urban park. They headed toward the playground and got situated at an empty park bench that overlooked the swings, which were largely empty except for a small handful of parents pushing their babies, likely trying to lull them into an afternoon nap.

"I don't miss those days. Dave and I used to take turns pushing Cooper for an hour trying to get him to relax and take a nap." Jen removed the plastic from her tofurkey wrap and took a bite. "So, how's Ravi?"

"Jen, how do you eat tofurkey?" Shauna shook her head. "That's just frickin' nasty. Either eat the real stuff or forgo it altogether. Fake meat should not be a thing."

"C'mon, Shauna." Jen chuckled. "I just wanted to mix it up. Plus, it's not *that* bad. Are you avoiding my question?"

"No." Shauna gave Jen a sidelong glance. "Things are good with Ravi. We're moving in together."

"Wow! That's a big step."

"Yeah, I'm excited." Shauna beamed and took a bite of her turkey wrap. "It will be a good test. Our parents are not so excited."

"When I moved in with Dave, our parents were totally against it, too, but they got over it. And living together helped me see all of Dave's, uh . . . shall we say, finer qualities?"

They both laughed. The last parent loaded their sleeping baby into the stroller and waved at Jen and Shauna when she passed them. Jen found herself staring at the empty swings, trying to remember the last time she took the kids to their neighborhood park. She made a mental note to make that a priority once the kids felt better and the next time the weather was nice.

"So, I wanted to talk to you about a new technology I just heard about." Shauna broke Jen's train of thought and put her wrap on the napkin in her lap. "I think it could automate a lot of what our benefits team does. I know it's not the right time to ask for money, but I think we should take a look."

Jen peeled back the plastic around her wrap. "Okay, let's take a look."

"Well, it's just that . . . wait, what?!"

"I said, sure, let's take a look. What's the big deal, Shauna?"

"I had a whole speech prepared. You never say yes right away."

"You're right and I'm sorry." Jen sighed. "This is clearly a passion for you, and I'm realizing that we have to experiment more with technologies."

"That's so cool."

"Good. Hey, by the way"—Jen swallowed the last bite of her wrap—"the sales team is evaluating a new employee engagement technology. Would you like to be involved in the pilot?"

"Yes." Shauna took a sip of water. "I'd love to be a part of it."

"Great. I'm excited to hear your thoughts."

"How's the family?" Mark smiled across the conference table in his office during their regular Friday catch-up. The warm weather had been an anomaly, and the rain was back, pelting the windows in his office.

"Good now—finally." Jen had a look of relief on her face. "Thanks for asking."

"They're such little germ spreaders at that age." Mark chuckled and shook his head. "My kids were always sick. Then Leanne and I would get it, and the Francis household would be down for weeks."

"Yep!" Jen exclaimed. "It happens in the Schmidt house too. We just lucked out this time."

They both laughed. Jen reclined in her chair, and Mark was pleased that she seemed to relax a bit. Jen had coached him to be more approachable during his one-on-one meetings with his direct reports. She gave him feedback that he was completely focused on the business and ran these meetings according to a strict agenda, which left her and many of the other leaders slightly disengaged. Over the past year, she had worked with him to show his human side and genuinely engage with his team, even when there was constant pressure on the business. He simply hadn't realized how he'd been coming across due to being too consumed with adjusting to his role as the new CEO.

"So . . ." Mark lightly tapped his fingers on the table. "I have a few things for you, but why don't you start with your list?"

"Sure. I wanted to update you on the SeeMe pilot." Jen opened a file folder. "Rich set up a demo for me and Shauna earlier this week. It looks like a viable solution. I told Rich that Shauna will stay involved."

"Was he okay with that?"

"Kind of." Jen laughed, tapping the table with her pen. "I assured him we wouldn't slow anything down."

"Okay, keep me posted," Mark requested. "I want you to stay close to this. I also talked to Rich about not going behind your back in the future. We have to stick together as a team if we're going to succeed. There are too many forces working against us to do this any other way."

"Thanks, Mark." Jen smiled. "I made a few changes on the HR side so this doesn't happen again."

"Really?" Mark leaned forward. "Like what?"

"I formed a small taskforce." Jen handed Mark a write-up. "Shauna will lead and partner with our IT team. They'll research the latest HR technologies and make recommendations."

"Terrific!" Mark skimmed her handout.

"I'm also working on a new process to solve problems. We have to practice what we preach."

"How did that go over with your team?"

"As expected." Jen shook her head with a knowing smile. "They were concerned about budgets with so many cutbacks. I explained that we invest in things that help us achieve our business goals."

"I get how that's confusing," Mark acknowledged, "but it sounds like you handled it well."

"Yeah, and I took your advice," Jen said softly. "Shauna and I are working on a plan for the team. It's clear we need to let people go in the next few weeks because they aren't going to be able to adapt to the new strategy."

"Let me know what you need from me." Mark folded his hands on the desk. "It's hard, but we'll be fair."

Jen and Mark continued to work through the items on their respective lists. They finished about a half hour later, and Jen stood up to leave.

"Good meeting. Just one more thing." Mark stood up from the table. "I told you the Cubs didn't have what it takes to make it to the World Series this year—"

"Ugh, Mark!" Jen threw her head back and looked at the ceiling. "Way to rub salt in the wound! I can't believe we lost the wildcard game. I'm not over it—and don't even *think* about talking to Michelle about it."

"In the end, it came down to what we said: the Cubs weren't consistent," Mark continued. "One day, the pitching was great—the next, their offense was great. But it was rare that they came together as a team."

"And I suppose you're going to tell me that the Red Sox were the perfect definition of a team?" Jen rolled her eyes. "You're so predictable."

Mark laughed. "Well, we made it! We may have been shaky at times, but if we can hold it together, we'll have a real chance to take it all home this year."

"We'll see." Jen stood up and gathered her papers and folders. "But I just have to say, you don't wear victory well. It's not pretty to watch."

Mark smirked. "I take it you're not rooting for my team, then?"

"Gotta stay true to the National League." Jen grinned. "Dodgers all the way!"

CHAPTER 11

"I CAN'T BELIEVE we're *really* here." Jen tugged Michelle's short-sleeve Cubs jersey in excitement on a Saturday afternoon late that fall. "This is the closest I've ever been to the actual field at Wrigley!"

After the Cubs' wildcard loss, Michelle had come up with the idea that she and Jen should take an off-season tour of Wrigley Field. They'd get to walk on the field, go to the dugout, see the visitors' clubhouse, and check out other key places at the historic stadium they both revered.

"I can't believe we've lived here our whole lives and haven't done this!" Michelle exclaimed. "How could we have missed this opportunity?"

They couldn't have picked a better afternoon. It was a warm, sunny day, with the temperature hitting the high sixties by lunchtime. They dressed for the occasion in their baseball jerseys, jeans, and Cubs hats and posed for pictures with a view of the famous field behind them.

"This is the perfect break! I've been stuck on this engagement survey for days." Jen smiled at her friend. "I can't figure out how to get people to fill it out. We've only got a week left, and nearly eighty percent of the company hasn't taken it."

Michelle rolled her eyes. "Why are you bringing up work right now? Live in the moment! We're on the tour of a lifetime!"

"Yeah, of course, sorry!" Jen shook her head. "Not sure what came over me."

The guide ushered them into the Cubs dugout and climbed up on the bench so everyone in the group could see him. Jen and Michelle were directly in front of him. "Does anyone have any questions?"

A gentleman in his seventies, dressed in jeans and a blue, long-sleeve Cubs T-shirt, raised his hand just above his head. "I was born and raised here, but I left Chicago when I was twenty-five. I actually have a general question about baseball these days. It seems very different from back in the day when I used to come to games here. I always see teams look at different-colored cards during the game. What are those?"

"Way to throw me a hard ball!" The guide smiled. "You know, it has to do with the data and analytics teams use. I'm no expert, but I'll do my best . . ."

"I'm sure you know more than I do." The gentleman chuckled. "My grandkids just made me get a cell phone!"

The entire tour laughed.

"The simplest way for me to explain it is those are actually cheat sheets the teams develop based on data and analytics." The tour guide flipped the access badge attached to a Cubs lanyard resting on his chest. "They have teams of computer experts that break down every play, every batter, and then analyze each aspect. They then put key information on those cards that guides the team on exactly what plays to make to maximize their chances of success. Does that help, sir?"

"Yes, it does. Thank you."

The tour guide smiled and jumped off the chair, signaling to the group to keep moving to the next stop on the tour—the visitors' clubhouse. "This way, everyone."

Jen stood perfectly still while the rest of the tour rushed past her and followed the guide. "The color-coded cards! I can't believe I didn't see it," she muttered quietly. She looked around the dugout, ideas spinning in her head.

Michelle gently touched Jen's arm. "You coming?"

"Totally!" Jen tried to focus on the moment but kept finding herself thinking about the engagement survey as they walked to the visitors' clubhouse.

The tour concluded about thirty minutes later, and the two women spent a few minutes buying souvenirs. After that, they made their way to Sheffield Avenue and walked for a couple minutes until they arrived at the legendary brick building with the green canopy—Murphy's Bleachers. Given that it was the off-season, the place was empty except for a few other small groups that had also been on the tour. Jen and Michelle waved to a few fellow fans and then made themselves comfortable on two green leather barstools at a round highboy table not too far from the bar. Michelle ordered two Old Style beers and some appetizers.

"Here's to a perfect day!" Michelle lifted her mug.

"Cheers!" Jen smiled at her friend. "This was a fantastic idea! We should do this every year from now on!"

They clinked glasses and each took a large gulp of cold beer.

"I think my favorite part was that bird's-eye view of the field. Just think about all the legendary players who have swung a bat or caught a fly ball on that field." Michelle squeezed ketchup on her french fries. "What about you?"

"That's a tough one. I loved every moment." Jen put her chicken wing down and turned to scan the autographed Cubs jerseys framed over the bar. "If I had to pick one moment, it was probably standing in the dugout. I loved the gentleman who asked about the cards. He was so cute."

"Yeah, he was. Especially when he pulled out his cell phone! Reminded me of my father-in-law." Michelle took a sip of her beer.

"His question about the analytics actually made me realize I've been thinking backwards about a few things." Jen bit into her chicken wing.

"Really? Like what?"

Jen hesitated, not wanting to ruin the moment. "Well, is it okay if I talk about work for a sec?"

"Sure." Michelle patted her stomach. "I've got a good base layer of beer and fried food in me, and we're surrounded by Cubs memorabilia in Wrigleyville—I think I can handle a little work talk."

Jen laughed and wiped her lip with her napkin. "After the tour guide reminded me how baseball teams use analytics to help them figure out the best plays, it occurred to me that I've been thinking about the engagement survey the wrong way. I've been solely focused on completion, and I think I may have missed the fact that the questions just aren't relevant."

"How so?" Michelle signaled to the waiter to bring another round of beers.

"Truth is, our survey isn't designed to collect relevant data. The questions are standard issue. They aren't tied to our business goals. We're not asking the right questions to get to the right information."

"Hmm . . . I know I filled it out." Michelle smiled at the waiter as he dropped of their beers. "I can't remember. I think I just felt like it was one of those HR things I *had* to do."

"Exactly." Jen picked up an onion ring. "And that's the problem. Rich's SeeMe pilot is going much better than the survey. I just looked at the dashboard yesterday, and now I get that he has the color-coded cards that baseball teams have. SeeMe collects the right data and analyzes it to give him real actions he can use to make a difference."

"Yeah, I had lunch with him last week, and he was pretty excited." Michelle took a bite of her chicken wing. "I was going to put some time on Shauna's calendar next week to talk about whether it could work for ops too."

"Cool!" Jen smiled. "I also have to rethink how we collect data. One of the great things about SeeMe is it integrates into everyday activities. It's not something people have to log into and fill out like my survey. It's just part of their workday."

"See, I told you this tour was exactly what we needed! We should tackle world peace next!" Michelle chuckled and stood up from her barstool. "But first, we're going to need some more food. I'm going to grab a menu from the bar. Be right back!"

"Thanks for inviting me to lunch, Allan." Jen glanced around the crowded, noisy Texas-themed steakhouse the following Monday a little after noon. "I can't remember the last time we did this."

"Hmm . . ." Allan stroked his chin. "Yeah, we used to go all the time back in the day at L&F. And even when you first started here, we had a good run for a bit. It's been too long."

"You make us sound so old with your 'back in the day' talk!" Jen placed her napkin on her lap and glanced at a menu. "But I agree, it's been too long. I guess we've both been busy."

"Yes." Allan put on his reading glasses and picked up his menu. "It has been crazy lately."

Jen stared at the stuffed moose head mounted on the wall. The eyes seemed to be looking right back at her. She shuddered a bit. "This place has such interesting décor. I feel like I am at a dude ranch."

"Yeah, but we're not dressed for it." Allan chuckled, pointing to his powder blue, patterned dress shirt and khaki pants. "But the food is pretty good. Have you been here before?"

"Yep—don't laugh." Jen shook her head. "Dave brought me here last year for a date night."

"Here?!" Allan's head popped back in surprise. "Oh, Davey, my boy! I gotta teach you a little about romantic settings."

Jen rolled her eyes. "He definitely could use the help."

"Good afternoon," the waitress interjected cheerfully. "What can I get you two today?"

"I'll have the steak salad lunch special." Jen handed the menu back to the waitress. "Medium well, please, with dressing on the side."

"Same for me," Allan added. "Thank you. So, Jen . . ." He took a sip of his iced tea as the waitress headed back to the kitchen. "Um, I wanted to talk a bit. Can we keep this conversation confidential? I mean, this can't go anywhere—not to Mark or Meg or anyone else for that matter."

"Of course." Jen was concerned. "Is everything okay?"

"Yeah, yeah, everything's fine." Allan glanced around the restaurant uncomfortably. "I just . . . well, something's come up, and I could use your advice."

"Sure." Jen took a sip of her water. "What's up?"

"Well, it's just, um . . . I'm being pursued." Allan coughed into his hand. "By another company. They want me to be their CFO."

"Oh." Jen's eyes widened, and she felt her heart start to race. "I see. And you're interested in what they have to say?"

"Well, I don't know. That's why I wanted to talk with you."
Allan played with his fork. "I mean, it's this group of investors
I know well. They've got an interesting opportunity at one of
their portfolio companies that has an innovative health product
on the consumer side. There's potential to make a lot of money
in a short period of time."

"Is that what you're looking for?" Jen could barely hear
herself speak over her pounding heart. Allan was such a pivotal
part of Dominal's leadership team. Just last week, she and Mark
had discussed how central he was to the company's growth
strategy. His departure would threaten their ability to meet
their six-month targets and be a huge setback for Dominal long
term, not to mention a big loss for Jen personally.

"It's not the only thing. But I admit, it piqued my interest. I
haven't done anything on the consumer side."

"Of course." Jen tried to project calmness and
professionalism.

"You know, the B2C would round out my experience and
resume." Allan went on. "Besides, once we've hit the six-month
targets, I just don't know what's next. It feels like my job is going
to be a bit more . . . well, you know, *predictable*. You know me, I
live for the battle, the next big thing. The money's hard to pass
up, but the challenge is what's most attractive. Do you think I
should consider it?"

"Allan, I can't . . ." Jen paused to collect her nerves and tried
a smile. "You and I both know the only person that can answer
that question is you."

Allan nodded slowly.

"Look, you know you're critical to Dominal, and I genuinely enjoy working with you, but I only want what's best for you—both personally and professionally. And I speak for Mark and the rest of the leadership team when I say we'd never want to hold you back."

"Yeah, I know that." Allan looked down. "But I'm having trouble figuring out what's next. I mean, what do you see down the road for me here at Dominal?"

Jen inhaled deeply as she processed Allan's question.

"Well, first, we're still in this battle of our company's life right now. It'd be a tough time for our CFO to depart. And then, once we do hit these targets, we both know there's still a lot of work ahead to get our market position back and meet our growth objectives. That's going to require innovative thinking from all of us. You're an integral part of that effort."

"True." Allan slightly tipped his head in a quick thank-you to the waitress when she put his salad on the table and refilled his iced tea.

Jen gave the waitress a half smile before continuing. "Do you remember at L&F, how we were always reacting to things?"

"Yeah, of course." Allan grabbed a sugar packet and lightly shook it. "But not just there, practically everywhere I've worked."

"Right." Jen picked up her fork. "Dominal is different. Mark is pushing us to think more broadly. We're building something unique and sustainable here. We're consciously rethinking everything—from our products, to how we delight our customers, to how we do HR and finance. Nothing's off the table. I think that's exciting. It certainly keeps the job interesting, even if the days are long."

"Agreed." Allan poured dressing over his salad. "But do you really think it offers the same types of challenges as what we've experienced during this turnaround period?"

"That's a good question." Jen nervously pushed her salad around her plate. "Look, I think like we lost our position in the market because we got complacent. We focused on the familiar, the routine, the predictable. Things like innovation and employee engagement were forgotten. We stopped challenging ourselves to find new ways to get things done."

Allan's expression indicated he agreed with Jen. He took another bite of his salad.

"Look"—Jen covered her mouth with her hand—"we need people like you on our leadership team, people who thrive on the challenge and will make sure we don't get sidetracked again."

"Well, you're speaking my language." Allan sipped his iced tea. "And that's why I'm conflicted."

"Well, maybe you need more specifics on what that looks like for you." Jen dabbed at the edges of her mouth with her napkin.

"Yeah, that'd help." Allan dipped a piece of steak in his remaining salad dressing. "You know, I value both your friendship and your guidance as head of HR."

They were both quiet for a moment as they dug into their lunch. Jen scanned the room uncomfortably; the rush of the lunch crowd had dwindled, leaving the restaurant a bit quieter.

But the only thing Jen could hear was the sound of her heart beating loudly against her chest. The thought of Allan leaving the company was crushing her personally and professionally and could spell the end of Dominal. She had to figure out something.

"Well . . ." Jen broke the silence. "If you do decide to pursue this, you should talk to Mark before you do anything. It's a small world, and he's going to find out—or worse, someone on the board will hear about it, and we'll lose the trust we've spent so much time building. Give him a chance to get ahead of it, okay?"

"Yeah, I hear you." Allan sighed and sat back in the booth, resting his arm across the top. "It'd be a hard conversation, but I know you're right. I guess I just gotta think about everything some more. Thanks for listening."

"You bet." Jen choked down a small bite of her salad, still feeling emotional from the potential loss of Allan. "I'm always here if you want to talk, and I promise I won't say anything to anyone."

"Okay. Onward, my friend." Allan smiled. "On another note, how's the engagement survey going? Are you getting good traction?"

"Not really." Jen sipped her water. "I realized it's not the tool for us going forward. There are more effective ways of getting insight on our engagement that, you know, would be more actionable. I'll keep you posted. They're likely cheaper too."

"You know that's music to a finance man's ears!" Allan laughed. "Of course you do—you're married to a finance guy."

"Yes, I married him *despite* the fact that he works in finance."

"Touché!" Allan grinned. "Will you excuse me a moment? I need to go to the little boy's room."

"Yeah, of course."

Once Allan left the booth, Jen pushed her lunch aside. She was nauseated thinking about their conversation. She went to reach for her phone to text Meg and remembered her promise to Allan.

"Crap!" she muttered to herself.

It was raining hard when Jen left the office at four o'clock. She was drenched and freezing cold by the time she got into her car. Once she got home, the first thing she did was take off her suit and towel-dry her hair. Desperate to warm up, she pulled on the new Cubs sweatshirt she'd purchased, a pair of cozy sweatpants, and her UGGs.

She made her way downstairs to the family room, where she built a fire and squeezed an oversized pillow, replaying the day's events in her head. She wanted to think a bit before Dave and the kids came home. The conversation with Allan was weighing on her. She had to work through a strategy. What was she going to say to Mark if Allan was serious about this new opportunity?

The front door flew open, and the kids came running into the house with Dave right behind them.

"Hi, honey. What a storm! Let me get them out of their wet clothes. I'll be down in a few." Dave took the kids upstairs and emerged in dry sweats and a sweatshirt a few minutes later.

"How did your meeting go with Regina?" Jen asked Dave, who was bending down into the refrigerator, picking out vegetables for the salad he was making for their dinner.

"Great!" Dave exclaimed. "They're going to consider me for Tanya's job."

"That's great!" Jen kissed Dave's cheek. "I'm so happy for you."

"Thanks, but I couldn't have done it without your guidance. Your advice to be curious was brilliant!" Dave set the ingredients on the kitchen island. "How was lunch with Allan?"

"Damn!" A hot, metal pot lid crashed down on the light blue ceramic tile.

"You all right?" Dave looked concerned.

Jen shot him a tense smile. "Yeah. Just burned my hand. I'm fine."

"Are you okay?" Dave was chopping carrots. "You seem pretty tense. Do you want to talk about it?"

"No," Jen barked. "I just want to have a nice dinner with my family."

"Okay." Dave cracked a PBR and took a sip. "But it may be hard with that tone."

"Yeah, I know." Jen shook her head, and her tone softened. "I'm sorry. I'd love to talk, but I just can't yet."

"Not even with me?" Dave made a goofy face as he washed radishes in the island sink. "Isn't there such a thing as marital privilege?"

"Probably." Jen sighed with a weary smile. "But I promised not to say anything, and I feel like I need to honor that. This one's a doozy."

"You know you can trust—" Dave was cut off by Kat and Cooper running into the kitchen.

"We're playing Dora the Exploser!" Kat cried. "I'm Dora and Coop is Boots."

"I'm not Boots. I'm Diego!" Cooper exclaimed. "Mommy, I keep telling her it's *explorer*, not *exploser*."

Jen couldn't help but smile. "Kitty Kat, your brother is right—it's *ex-plor-er*. Can you try to say that?"

"That's what I said!" Kat bobbed her head up and down enthusiastically. "*Exploser*."

Jen felt her stress starting to melt away. She'd spent enough time on the Allan situation for the day. Now it was family time.

"Dinner's almost ready," Dave announced. "How about Dora and Diego go wash their hands?"

Jen took the chicken out of the oven and put the dish on the table. On her way back to the kitchen, Dave squeezed her arm. "Try your best to relax. It's all going to be okay."

"From your lips to God's ears." Jen cast her eyes up to the white ceiling.

"You wanted to see me?" Jen knocked lightly on Mark's office door right after lunch on Wednesday afternoon. The early winter sky darkened his office considerably, and Mark had turned on all the lights to compensate.

"Yes, come in, and please shut the door." Mark's tone was serious. He gestured to the guest chair. "Have a seat."

"Are you okay?"

"Not really. I just talked to Allan. He told me there's a company pursuing him. He said he talked to you about it."

"Yes, he asked me to keep it confidential." Jen glanced at the light snowfall outside. "I hope you understand I felt I had to honor his trust."

"I'm not going to lie, I'm annoyed!" Mark shook his head. "A heads-up would have been nice."

"Look, it wasn't an easy decision." Jen narrowed her eyes, taken aback by Mark's comments. "Allan and I have known each other for years. He hadn't taken any action yet, and he specifically asked me not to say anything to you. I did what I felt was right. But I also strongly encouraged him to talk to you before doing anything. I take it this means he put his hat in the ring?"

"I am trying *really* hard not to be annoyed. I know you two go way back, and it's a tough spot." Mark closed his eyes. "Allan isn't sure. He wanted my opinion. I'm not going to lie, it was awkward."

"What did you tell him?" Jen braced herself and refocused her gaze on Mark.

"You know, the same thing as you." Mark bit the earpiece of his glasses. "We don't hold people back here—but what a huge loss for us if he leaves. If he decides to pursue this opportunity, I'll have to talk to Renata. It would be catastrophic if this news got back to the board. I'd have to manage it proactively."

"Agreed." Jen wrung her hands. "It would destroy the trust we've built with them over the past few months."

"Don't you think we should just pay him more?" Mark stood up and began pacing behind his desk. "I mean, he's worth every penny."

"I'm not sure that will do it. Do you really want someone who has one foot out the door as your CFO right now?"

"It will buy us the time we need to hit our goals," Mark argued. "We need that."

"I want Allan to stay more than anything, but we're not going to hit our six-month targets unless he's one hundred percent committed and engaged."

"Shit, Jen!" Mark punched his hand. "What the hell are we going to do?"

"I know. I haven't slept for two nights." Jen rubbed her temples. "But did you really listen to him? It's not just the money. We have to figure out a clear way to show him what his future looks like here. He wants to solve big problems. He wants to innovate."

"Yeah, he mentioned something about that." Mark picked up a pen and flung it on the desk. "Jesus! At least if we offer him a raise, we'll know a bit more from his reaction, right?"

"I disagree." Jen made sure her voice did not waver. "We both need to calm down and think creatively about how to paint an attractive picture for Allan."

"Did you talk to Meg about this?"

"No, I didn't even talk to Dave about it." Jen sighed. "Allan asked for complete confidentiality. It's been tearing me apart."

"I asked him to let me know by Monday." Mark stood completely still, facing Jen. "Hey, you're a painter, aren't you?"

"I am . . ." Jen cocked her head.

"Well, then—paint the best picture you can of Allan's future life at Dominal." Mark looked out into the gloom. "Something compelling. Something that'll help him make the right decision."

"I will." Jen stood up to leave. "Keep me posted on what you hear."

———⚬———

Jen sat down at the dining room table at around half past eight that same evening. The kids were tucked in, and Dave was upstairs working in their bedroom. She had spent the rest of the afternoon carefully reviewing her strategy and thinking through how to appeal to Allan and engage his head and heart in hopes that her friend and colleague would stay with Dominal.

She took a deep breath, searching for inspiration. Struggling, she soaked in the colors and angles of her dozen or so paintings that lined the room. She remembered how she had worked so hard to capture the unique perspectives of the Windy City's landmarks, at least how she saw them through her own lens. She wished she had more time for painting these days. It always helped with the stress.

"Okay, let's do this . . ." she whispered as she turned on her laptop. She opened a new email, typed in Allan's address, and began writing:

Dear Allan,

I wish that I had the courage to have this conversation with you in person. Please forgive me that I can't right now. I'm too torn.

I've been thinking a lot about what you asked me at lunch—what would your life would look like at Dominal after we hit our targets? What would be the next big thing to keep you excited and engaged?

To be honest, a few months ago, I would have given you a textbook answer—maybe made a few gestures to entice you: a fancy new title and pay to match. And we could still do that, but we both know that won't address your concerns.

I now understand that textbook solutions have short-term results. We both know that our current competitive pressures and an onslaught of new technologies present an existential threat to Dominal. This requires long-term thinking and solutions.

Though I've been with Dominal for nearly two years, it's only been in the past few months—with Meg's coaching—that I have really started to "get" that these threats are actually opportunities . . . very exciting ones, in fact. Let me explain.

You know that we are redesigning how work gets done at Dominal. My team and I are driven to create a work environment filled with *possibility and opportunity, a place where no one has to ask, "What if?" because experimentation and new ideas are constantly being tested—no matter how bold they are. Every single person at Dominal will have the power to innovate and make a difference.*

How different would it be to be part of a leadership team where THIS is the mindset? Imagine working at a place where you are not only creatively challenged every single day, but everyone around you is as well. Think of the amazing culture, products, and team we could build! We could transform Dominal into a powerful company that shapes our industry.

Should you stay with Dominal, you'd play a significant role in this. You're such a force when it comes to these types of big challenges, and you want to innovate, which makes you uniquely qualified to be a key partner in leading this transformation.

No matter what you decide, you know I will always support you 100%. First and foremost, you are my friend. I only want what's best for you, Mindy, and the kids. But just to be clear, this place wouldn't be the same without you. I mean, let's be real, Bananarama's "Baby It's Christmas" is something ONLY Allan Chang can cover during holiday karaoke! ☺

If you're open to a conversation, I have specific initiatives and targets laid out for the first year. I'm happy to dive into the details with you. Let me know your thoughts.

Thanks,

Jen

Jen sat back at the dining room table and reread the email a few times to make sure she'd hit all the key points. On her fourth reread, she yawned and looked at the clock—ten thirty. It was now or never. She said a silent prayer and pressed send.

———— ◇ ————

"Will you look at that *ring*?! Oh, Shauna, it's beautiful." Jen opened her arms and gave Shauna a huge hug. "Congratulations! We are so happy for you!"

"Thanks, Jen." Shauna stood against the island in Jen's kitchen on a blustery Saturday evening. She glanced down at the sparkling diamond ring on her left hand. "Ravi and I decided we weren't comfortable moving in together unless we were engaged."

Jen turned back to the stove to check on dinner. "Have you set a date?"

"We're not going to wait too long. We just want our wedding to be a simple, fun day for friends and family." Shauna sipped her tequila. "It really depends on venues and auspicious dates for Ravi's side of the family. We're hoping for spring."

"That's four months away!" Jen stirred a pot of sauce. "Are you going to do an Indian wedding? Those are so beautiful."

"Probably a hybrid of some sort. Neither of us is religious, but we want to incorporate both of our cultures."

"It's going to be amazing no matter how you do it," Jen said. "It's your day. Remember, it's about what you and Ravi want. Nothing else matters."

"Thanks." Shauna seemed to be glowing. The two continued to make small talk about Shauna's initial thoughts on the wedding ceremony while Jen floated around the kitchen getting dinner ready.

"Hey, not to bring up work, but one quick thing. I can't believe Mark signed off on the new technology pilots. The taskforce is thrilled."

Jen turned away from the stovetop. "You guys presented some compelling stuff."

"Well, you helped guide us." Shauna beamed and glanced around at the artwork in the adjoining family room. Jen felt her stomach tighten the way it always did when somebody outside of her family viewed her work. "Is this painting of Wrigley Field new? I love the angles."

"Well, I painted it after we won the World Series, but we just got around to hanging it up a few weeks ago." Jen tossed the salad. "Will you take this to the dining table for me? I don't know where Dave went."

"He and Ravi are in the basement. I'm sure they're talking about whatever guys talk about."

"Their own version of shop talk in the man cave? I should have never given into the oak bar and sixty-inch, flat-screen TV." Jen searched around for her wine glass and finally found it next to the stove. "I'm glad they're getting along."

"Me too." Shauna grinned. "So, were Kat and Cooper disappointed they didn't get to hang with Auntie Shauna and Uncle Ravi tonight?"

"Ugh, Dave and I were bad parents." Jen feigned regret. "We played up spending the night at their grandparents' house and conveniently left out that you were coming over. They would have never left!"

"They are the sweetest." Shauna smiled. "I love spending time with them."

Jen opened the oven door and checked the roast. "It doesn't help that Auntie Shauna brings toys *every* time she visits."

"Kids deserve a little love."

"Hmm . . ." Jen refilled her wine glass. "We'll see how your perspective changes over time."

"Hey, how was lunch with Allan?" Shauna asked. "You two were gone for a few hours."

"Yeah." Jen froze for a moment at the stove, the stress of the Allan incident draining the color from her face. She shook her head slightly to regain her composure and return to Shauna. "You know, just reminiscing a bit on L&F and catching up on old colleagues. It's been a while since we had quality time together."

"Totally." Shauna adjusted her sweater. "I bet it was nice to catch up. Was the food good? I've been wondering about that steakhouse . . ."

Jen's phone buzzed with a text. "Sorry, Shauna, just give me a sec."

The text was from Mark: *Allan not pursuing it. Said the picture you painted made all the difference. Great work! Thx.*

Jen expelled a sigh of relief and texted back: *Great news!*

"What are you so happy about?" Shauna asked.

"Nothing, just a bit of good news that I was waiting for." Jen exhaled, took a big gulp of wine, and smiled at Shauna. "Where were we?"

"Well, new topic—I'm curious, what were Mark's comments about the team plan we put together?"

"He gave us the go-ahead to start letting people go next week."

"Okay, that's good, I guess." Shauna sighed deeply. "Ugh, I don't want to think about that tonight, do you?"

"No, next week will be hard," Jen acknowledged and lifted her glass. "But tonight is about celebrating your engagement! Dave and I are so happy for you."

"Thanks, Jen." Shauna lifted her glass as well. "It's really nice of you guys—I mean, *you*—to cook!"

"We're super excited." Jen lightly squeezed Shauna's arm.

"Yeah." Shauna looked down at her ring and beamed. "I still can't believe it's happening."

CHAPTER 12

"THESE PAINTINGS ARE amazing, my friend!" Meg glanced around Jen's dining room in the late afternoon of a perfect spring Friday in March. "Zoom doesn't do them justice."

"Thanks!" Jen smiled. "I'm so glad you made it to Chicago. I know it will mean a lot to Shauna to have you at her big day tomorrow."

"I can't believe she pulled a whole wedding together in four months! I wouldn't miss it. You know I think Shauna's awesome! Plus, this is the best time of year to visit." Meg studied the paintings one by one. "Hey, is that the Sears Tower?"

"Yeah, actually, it goes by Willis Tower now. I took a bunch of pictures from different angles and tried to put it together."

"That's right, Willis Tower! You really have a gift!" Meg smiled. "So, I know we said no work today, but I'm curious about Thursday's board meeting."

"It was great!" Jen exclaimed. "We actually exceeded our six-month targets, and the board is ecstatic about our progress. Juanita has hit the ground running. Also, I forgot to tell you, our Glassdoor rating is up to 3.9."

"Terrific!" Meg eyes widened. "How do you feel?"

"You know, for the first time I feel like I'm making a real impact, and everyone sees HR's value. Even Rich partners with us now. He has such great insight on customer acquisition, which our team has used to inform our recruiting strategy. I'm glad we figured out a way to work together."

"That's terrific. I knew you could do it!"

"Well, I didn't do it alone." Jen grinned. "You really steered us. I can't thank you enough for everything you've done. I'm excited for our next adventure."

"My pleasure." Meg beamed. "I look forward to seeing what's next for you and Dominal.

"Here you go, Meg!" Dave walked into the living room and handed her a PBR. "Thanks for making the time to come over for dinner."

"Thanks for having me. I've heard so much about you." Meg took a sip of her PBR. "Oh well, that's . . . uh . . . I didn't remember it tasting so much like water!"

Jen and Dave laughed.

"Seriously, I'm excited to spend quality time with the famous *Dave*." Meg raised her beer to toast Dave.

"Well, I heard you worked in finance for a bit of your career. And clearly we appreciate the finer beers in life!" Dave teased. "So I am sure our great minds think alike!"

"Whatever, you two!" Jen rolled her eyes. "Have a seat, Meg. We have a few minutes before Dave's parents drop the kids back home, and then we won't have any quiet time."

———◦◦———

Jen and Dave mingled with the group gathering in the lavishly decorated hotel ballroom the following afternoon. The hotel was located right on the waterfront and had impressive views of Lake Michigan. The ballroom had floor-to-ceiling windows that let in plenty of natural light.

"Meg!" Jen walked toward Meg with her arms outstretched. "You look great! I love your dress. The pattern on the scarf is amazing—is it Indian?"

"Yes, thought I would add a dash of spice to the outfit, given the occasion." Meg studied the handsome couple in front of her. Dave wore a charcoal gray suit with a light blue shirt and red tie, while Jen wore a red dress with black stilettos. "Well, don't you and Dave clean up well!"

"Nice to see you again!" Dave hugged Meg. "Hope you recovered from the PBRs last night."

"Ha!" Meg chuckled. "Thanks again for dinner. I loved meeting Cooper and Kat!"

"And they loved Auntie Meg's gifts and stories!" Dave smiled. "Shall we find seats?"

Jen gestured toward a set of chairs. "I think Michelle and Joe are saving seats for us."

"This place looks amazing." Meg took in the view of the red and gold decorations that surrounded the stage where a small wedding Mandap had been constructed for the Indian portion of the ceremony. "Shauna and Ravi did a beautiful job."

"Totally. I know they were disappointed they couldn't have a real fire indoors because of safety rules, but this is still an ideal setting for a wedding. It will be memorable." Jen took out her phone. "Look, I took a few pictures of the Mandap from different angles. I want to try to paint it, especially with the view in the background."

"Oooh!" Meg took Jen's phone and scrolled through the pictures. "I can't wait to see it."

"What about you?" Jen asked when Meg handed her phone back. "Do you think you will write a poem about today?"

"I hope so." Meg smiled. "I'm definitely taking in all the sights and scenes."

"Cool. I am excited to read it!"

"Hey, Meg!" Michelle hugged her. "So nice to see you! Let me introduce you to my husband. Wait, where did Joe go?"

"So, he can't sit still either," Jen whispered to Meg. "I'm not exactly sure how they have a conversation."

Meg laughed. "Has Shauna made an appearance yet?"

"Not yet. I think they're doing the pre-wedding stuff for the Hindu ceremony right now. Let's sit down." Jen took Dave's hand and guided him toward the open seats while Meg followed.

"What are you writing, Meg?" Michelle took a sip of her Coors Light as the group waited for dinner to be served during the reception.

"Just capturing some thoughts in case inspiration hits."

"That's cool." Michelle nodded. "You know, a lot of things rhyme with *Michelle*, just in case you want to work me into a poem."

"Sure, like shell, tell, fell, sell, bell—"

"Don't forget *hell*," Jen chimed in.

They all laughed.

"You know, Meg"—Jen sipped her merlot—"Shauna really looks up to you. She soaks up everything you say like a sponge."

"Well, I think she looks up to you, too, Jen." Meg took a sip of her Half Acre Pony pilsner. "You're developing her well."

"Okay, enough of the mutual admiration society!" Michelle interjected and glanced at the head table where the newly wed-ded couple sat flanked by their immediate family. "Seriously, though, what a nice couple. I've always liked Ravi."

"Here's to the happy couple." Jen raised her glass, and the rest of the table clinked glasses.

"Meg . . ." Michelle turned to face her. "Can I ask you something?"

"Of course."

"I'm trying to figure you out." Michelle sat on the edge of her chair. "What made you leave corporate? Were you a creative who didn't fit, or was it something else?"

"That's a good question." Meg seemed to hesitate, then shrugged her shoulders. "I always felt like I had to hide my creative side. I never talked about my poetry—as a matter of fact, I denied I was a poet for years. I'm not even sure most of my friends knew."

"Why?" Jen asked. "Your poetry is such a huge part of who you are."

"Yes, but poets aren't exactly the happiest people in the world," Meg reasoned. "But I learned over time that if you try to suppress creativity, it overwhelms you."

"So, what were you like in corporate?" Jen sipped her merlot. "I can't imagine you wore suits every day."

"I sure did." Meg chuckled. "Put on that Tahari uniform every day—but there was always this nagging feeling that I was in someone else's skin."

"That's interesting." Jen looked at Michelle. "I just told Michelle that I was going to stop wearing suits to work. It's not who I am, and it's not Dominal. Hard to walk around a manufacturing facility in stilettos."

"Good for you." Meg took a gulp of beer. "You'll figure out what works over time. It took me a while after I left corporate to find my own voice."

"Well, we're glad you did." Michelle raised her glass, and Meg clinked it. "Say, Meg, do you coach non-HR people? I mean, I was thinking about asking Mark if I could work with you too."

"Sure. We can talk next week." Meg's expression became serious. "But Michelle, it will require you to sit still for a bit. Do you think you can handle it?"

"Yeah, that may be hard." Michelle smiled. "Do you do fifteen-minute blocks?"

They all laughed. The quiet, instrumental Indian music switched to a loud, fast-paced dance song, and guests started to make their way to the dance floor.

"Okay, I'm headed to the bar. Who's up for another round?" Michelle asked over the mix of Indian and Western dance music that had started to play. "Meg, I know you want to hydrate and switch to a Coors Light."

"Sure, why not?" Meg downed the rest of her pilsner. "I'm not driving!"

Michelle elbowed her way to the crowded bar and brought the women back a round of drinks. The group at the table watched Shauna and Ravi's friends crowd the dance floor for several minutes in silence.

"Oh, Meg—" Jen reached underneath her chair and pulled out a package. "I totally forgot. I have something for you. Open it."

Meg unwrapped package and pulled out a Chicago Cubs T-shirt.

"Ha!" Meg smiled and held it out. "I guess I have something new to wear to our virtual happy hours. Thank you."

"You can never have too much Cubs stuff in your wardrobe." Jen's eyes widened. "It just makes every outfit better."

"If you say so." Meg took a sip of her Coors Light and cringed. She turned to Jen. "Wow, that's rough after good beer. I don't know how Michelle drinks this stuff!"

"Hey!" Michelle exclaimed. "I heard that!"

They all laughed.

"Did you notice it's from the 2016 winning season?"

"No, I didn't. That's cool, Jen. Thanks."

"That series reminds me of our team at Dominal," Jen added. "You coached us through our own Game 7."

"Totally!" Michelle chimed in. "You remember, the Cubs were behind. Everything was stacked against them. Then, Jason Heyward used the rain delay to remind his teammates why they were the best in baseball. They came back and rallied to their historic win."

"Yeah, you're our J-Hey, Meg." Jen patted Meg on the back. "You helped us remember why Dominal is the best. We've got our confidence back thanks to you." Everyone raised their glasses toward Meg. "To Meg!"

"Thanks, guys." Blushing brightly, Meg raised her glass and turned to face Jen. "I propose another toast. I'd like us all to raise a glass to Jen. I might have been her coach, but she was the one who drove the transformation that enabled Dominal to achieve its goals. It's been amazing to watch you grow, my friend."

"To Jen," the group cheered with raised glasses.

Jen smiled back at Meg and mouthed, "Thank you."

EPILOGUE

EIGHTEEN MONTHS LATER

IT WAS A drizzly Thursday in September, and Mark sat at the desk in his home office after lunch with his head in his hands. It was the sixth month of the COVID-19 pandemic, which had changed everything about his life; he and his family were overwhelmed with everyone working and attending school from home. He looked up, sighed deeply, and proceeded to connect to his eighth Zoom call of the day.

"Hi, Renata. How are you? Jen's running a few minutes behind."

"I'm well, Mark. We're staying safe and healthy, which is about all you can hope for these days. I'd be doing better if schools were open. What about you?"

"Same here." Mark stood up and peered out his window at the dark gray sky enveloping his neighborhood. "Leanne and I are realizing how small our house is with everyone home."

"Is Jack still home from college?" Renata asked. "He must be disappointed."

"Yes, it's a bummer." Mark sighed. "Honestly, though, it's for the best—one less thing to worry about."

"We're definitely living in unusual times."

"Hi, everyone. Sorry I'm a little late." Jen face showed up on the screen. "We're having school challenges this afternoon."

"Oh, I can so relate!" Renata shook her head. "Yesterday I had to present at a virtual diversity conference, and the kids were so restless. I finally gave up and handed the kids iPads and told them to do whatever they wanted for the rest of the afternoon."

"Yep, that was us this morning." Jen frowned. "You gotta do what you gotta do."

Renata grinned. "So, let's dive in. The board had a chance to go through your bonus recommendations for the leadership team, and I wanted to give you some feedback on what you submitted for Allan, Rich, and Michelle."

"Okay." Mark braced himself. "What do you think?"

"Well, first, the board is very impressed with how you exceeded your goals this year. A short while ago, things were looking bleak, but today we've regained our position in the marketplace."

"Thanks, Renata. We're looking forward to our continued growth this year." Mark felt himself relax a bit.

"Your team has done a stellar job," Renata continued. "We feel like your recommendations take that into account. You can't lose this team. So, we approved the generous bonuses that you recommended for Allan, Rich, and Michelle."

"That's great!" Jen exclaimed. "Thank you, Renata."

"Yes. Thanks, Renata!" Mark was jubilant. "I will send a note to the other board members to thank them too."

"Mark, do you have time to call everyone this afternoon?" Jen asked. "I think they could use something to look forward to right now."

"Yes, of course, I'll definitely make time for that." Mark adjusted his glasses.

"If you have just a few extra minutes, Mark, I have one more thing to cover with you."

"No problem. Jen, I'll call you after I've spoken to the others."

"Okay." Jen smiled. "Thanks, Renata, and good luck with the homeschooling thing. Remember, the iPad is your friend right now!"

"Ha!" Renata laughed. "Thanks, Jen. Talk soon!"

"So, Mark, I wanted to talk to you about Jen's bonus," Renata started. "The board is making an adjustment to your recommendation."

"What's the issue?" Mark straightened up in his chair. "She has really transformed HR."

"No argument there." Renata motioned for Mark to relax. "Your turnover numbers have significantly improved, productivity was strong well before the pandemic, and we continue to be impressed with the quality of your team at all levels."

"So, then . . . I don't understand." Mark rubbed his forehead. "Why are they adjusting my recommendation?"

"The board actually felt it was too low. We'd like to increase your recommendation by fifteen percent."

"Oh, wow! Thanks." Mark's entire body relaxed. "That's terrific news."

"I also wanted to let you know that Dominal is the only company in the Gold portfolio who was ahead of the curve on the pandemic. The team saw what was happening in China and built a contingency plan."

"Yeah, I just had a feeling about it. Similar to what I was raising at D&E. But this time I was in control and could take action on it." Mark leaned back in his chair and looked out at the window. The drizzle had morphed into a full rain, and his view was obstructed by large droplets forming on the window. "Allan and Jen did some terrific analyses on potential scenarios."

"Good for you," Renata commented. "You know, sometimes leaders struggle to execute when they're the actual decision maker. I am glad that didn't happen to you."

"Look, everything I told D&E came true, and they're now defunct." Mark shook his head. "I wasn't about to let that happen to Dominal. I figured if this pandemic never hit the US, well, at least we had a disaster recovery plan for pandemics."

"Ha!" Renata laughed. "Because you can never have enough contingency plans."

"You really can't." Mark chuckled. "We also got lucky in that we were considered an essential business in some ways."

"Maybe—but some of the other essential businesses in our portfolio have struggled. Dominal continues to outperform."

"I'm excited." Mark propped his elbows up on the desk. "Despite COVID, this is going to be a record year."

"The board shares your excitement," Renata confirmed. "We're impressed by how you've taken care of your employees *and* kept the business growing. Productivity is steady, despite turbulent times. That's quite an accomplishment."

"Thanks, Renata." Mark smiled broadly. "A lot of that's Jen. She's really grown as a leader of HR and our business."

"Yeah, she really blossomed working with Meg." Renata agreed. "We've actually got Meg working with a few other clients in our portfolio and are seeing similar results."

"That's great."

"Well, congratulations, Mark! You know I've always believed in you right from the very start."

"Thanks, Renata, have a good one!" Mark disconnected from Zoom. He was thrilled at the news and excited to be making the next round of phone calls to his leadership team.

Immediately after disconnecting from the Zoom call with Mark, Renata picked up her cell phone and placed a call.

"Hi, Renata," Jen said, sounding a bit surprised. "Is everything okay?"

"Hi, Jen. Yes, I was just wondering if you had a few minutes to chat?"

"Of course. What can I do for you?"

"Listen, I understand this is all supposed to be confidential"—Renata paused—"but I know Allan was being pursued hard by another company to be their CFO."

"Yes. That caused a few sleepless nights." Jen sighed. "But it all worked out. He didn't even pursue it."

"Yes, I know," Renata rubbed her forehead. "I also know you played a key role in convincing him not to pursue it."

"I simply told him what we're building at Dominal and showed him his role in the bigger picture."

"Well, very fine work, Jen. Really. I think it would have been impossible for Dominal to be where it is today had he left. I wanted to thank you personally for turning things around. Mark told me you're quite a . . . painter." Renata smiled.

"Yes. I've certainly worked hard on the skill." Jen laughed. "At the end of the day, we're all just people pursuing our purpose. I'm the head of HR, so it's my job to be a resource for these people."

"I like it!" Renata exclaimed. "Tell me more."

"You know, it was Meg who helped me see this. She's a poet who has such a unique perspective and is a master at guiding leaders. And I couldn't have done this without Mark, who's an insightful leader that sees the implications of trends when others don't. Michelle's an influencer who can align people toward a common goal. Rich sees opportunities where others don't. And Allan, well, he's a creative problem solver who loves a challenge. This is the team that drives Dominal forward. It's my job to paint a clear, inviting picture of where this team of talented people is headed, right? So that's just what I did."

"Well, you really made it happen. Listen, Mark, Allan, and few board members are getting together for a virtual dinner this weekend—a casual celebration of Dominal's impressive comeback. Are you able you join us?"

"Renata . . . I'd love to join, and I agree that it was quite the comeback!"

THERE'S A BETTER WAY TO DO HR.

Resources, courses, and consulting at theloglab.net

HR FOR THE MODERN WORLD
www.theloglab.net

ACKNOWLEDGEMENTS

THANK YOU FOR taking the time to read this book. My goal was to write a book that I would enjoy reading. I have always been attracted to corporate fiction—stories that are engaging and fun to read but also provide valuable lessons, and I wanted to try my hand at that. I genuinely enjoyed developing the characters and piecing the story together. As you all know, writing a book is not a solo effort, and there are many people I must acknowledge who made this book possible.

First and foremost, I want to thank my editor, Kathy Meis, and her team at Bublish. From our first call, Kathy shared my excitement and enthusiasm for this book. She has been a wonderful guide, cheerleader, and writing coach. And she has also become a great friend.

I have always enjoyed storytelling. My parents told me that once I could talk, they would often observe me in my crib telling stories to the animals that decorated the walls of my bedroom. So, a special thanks to my mom, Sulbha, and my dad, Pramod, for always encouraging my creativity. And of course, my lifelong partner-in-crime, my big brother, Sachin, who was always willing to jump into any fantastical world that my imagination conjured up. I also want to thank my sister-in-law, Poonam, my niece, Saya, and my entire extended family for their continued love and support.

They say that your friends are your chosen family, and I am truly blessed with a wonderful group of close friends who support me unconditionally through life's ups and downs. I want to acknowledge a few who were instrumental in helping me with this book. Thanks to Shelye Potter, who over the last thirteen years has patiently listened and encouraged every zany idea I've had (including a book about HR, baseball, and beer) and always finds a meaningful way to contribute and help me achieve my goals. She and her mom, Lynn, introduced me to the Cubs and its unique culture in Chicago. I also want to acknowledge Mindy Amster and Adam Beechen, who have indulged all my ideas over the past eleven years and have been an amazing source of support. Their enthusiasm, guidance, and feedback were critical to my being able to write this book.

I'd also like to acknowledge all the beta readers who took the time to read a rough version of this book and gave me great feedback, which includes everyone I listed above, as well as Teuila Hanson, Dr. Cindi Gilliland, Viru Parlikar, Mikael Berner, Meg Stimson, Stephanie Hanson, Dr. Heather Backstrom, Ashleigh Kasper, and Ric Franzi.

I'd like to acknowledge my fantastic marketing team, Hunter Davis, Beau Morris, and the entire crew at Millennial Pixels who helped me find my voice after I left corporate and craft a unique brand around it. They always stand ready to support any business idea or direction and help me take something that's good in concept and make it into something memorable.

Finally, I'd like to thank everyone I've worked with over the past twenty-five years for sharing their stories and contributing to my experiences. Without you, this story wouldn't have been possible.